FINDING
PURPOSE IN ADVERSITY

Finding Purpose in Adversity

A Story of Survival, Hope, Redemption,
Life Lessons, and God's Unearned Grace.

Shannon McAteer, PhD
Major, United States Army (Retired)

Christina McAteer
Wonder Woman

XULON PRESS

Xulon Press
2301 Lucien Way #415
Maitland, FL 32751
407.339.4217
www.xulonpress.com

Unless otherwise indicated, Scripture quotations taken from the Holy
Bible, New Living Translation (NLT). Copyright©1996, 2004, 2007 by
Tyndale House Foundation. Used by permission of Tyndale House
Publishers, Inc.

Scripture quotations taken from the Holy Bible, New International
Version (NIV). Copyright © 1973, 1978, 1984, 2011 by Biblica, Inc.™.
Used by permission. All rights reserved.

Printed in the United States of America.

ISBN-13: 978-1-6305-0513-4

Dedication

W e dedicate this book to our parents: Elaine (Shannon's mother) and Bill and Pat (Christina's parents). While imperfect—like the rest of us—they were present, encouraging, and committed in their efforts to shape us into the persons we have become. We thank you so much for your love, commitment, and support.

Table of Contents

Chapter 1
Chapter 2
Chapter 3
Chapter 4
Chapter 5
Chapter 6
Chapter 7
Chapter 8
Chapter 9

Foreword

I n Hebrews 12:1–2, we read that our faith in Jesus can be compared to a race we run with endurance and focus. We can run the race because we have a group of witnesses cheering us on. The people along the route of our race are not spectators; they are witnesses. The difference between a spectator and a witness is one of experience.

Witnesses tell us about their own race of faith and how the grace of God kept them running their own race. Shannon and Christina McAteer are witnesses for me, my wife, and our children. They are persistent in their pursuit of God in all things. Their unfailing friendship is a testimony to God's goodness and the value of learning and growing despite life's many challenges.

In this book, Shannon testifies about God's goodness in his life with both venerability and wisdom. His story is one worth telling and one worth reading.

Joshua A. Fletcher, DMin
Pastor, Missionary, Artist

Preface

I served our nation in the United States Army for twenty-two years, and I spent half of my career in the 160th Special Operations Aviation Regiment (SOAR). In the SOAR, we specialize in capture or kill, and hostage rescue missions, and other types of specialized missions. The story here is about one of many missions I flew in Iraq.

Our mission was to capture or kill an enemy bomb maker who was known for killing Americans. These types of people are called high value targets (HVTs). The assignment was no different from many I flew before, but for some reason I was more nervous than usual. Perhaps it was due to my landing position—the front door of the HVT's home—and that I was in the pilot seat on the right, which put me adjacent to his front door. I envisioned terrorists charging out the front door, shooting down my aircraft with hundreds of bullets, and killing everyone on board.

As advanced as an MH-60 Blackhawk is, it is not heavily armored. Small arms, such as the 7.62mm rounds from an AK-47, can leave a Blackhawk looking like Swiss cheese—never mind Rocket Propelled Grenades (RPGs) that can do far worse damage. We did have mini-guns that could return fire at a rate of four thousand rounds a minute, but we were subject to a window of vulnerability because we had to locate targets before we could return fire. That vulnerability bothered me the most about that mission.

As we prepared to launch, I mapped out my approach to the landing area in my head. Helicopters would land all around the HVT's house, dropping off the best talent the United States had, including seasoned veterans we referred to as "customers" to try and protect their units' identities. The customers on my aircraft would get out of the helicopter and knock down the front door for maximum surprise. I had to be extremely precise in order to be at the landing zone for as little time as possible, safely get the customers on the ground, and then get back into relatively safe airspace afterward.

I planned an aggressive approach that would minimize exposure for my aircraft, passengers, and crew. We departed Ballad Airfield as a flight of four MH-60s and a full load of customers. We had an hour flight, so I ran through my approach into the target area over and over again in my mind. As we approached the release point (RP), everything moved faster. The RP is the last checkpoint before infiltration (infil) of the assault force, and everything happens in a very short period of time. There is only three to five kilometers—a couple minutes in flight time—between the RP and aircraft touchdown. At the RP, we slowed from 120 knots to 80 knots and eventually drop to zero at landing. We also had to turn the aircraft as we looked for our specific aircraft touchdown point and to ensure we landed at a very specific time—plus or minus thirty seconds of our planned arrival. Our goal was to beat the aircraft in front of us to the ground. Since we land into the wind to help with our aircraft power requirements, the wind blows whatever is in front of us, toward us. So, when the aircraft in front of us touches down, it kicks up dust and creates a brown-out condition that is difficult, and sometimes impossible, to see through. If we beat the aircraft in front of us to the ground, we land in semi-clear air and only have to deal with the dust we kick up.

After crossing the RP, I could see the HVT's house and then my landing area in his front yard. As I continued my final approach, I scanned for hazards, such as trees, powerlines, fences, and bad guys. I also watched the other aircraft in our formation and slowed my airspeed. The aircraft was not slowing enough, and my crew chief told me as much.

"Sir, you're coming in quite fast."

"Roger. Got it," I replied. But the helicopter still was not slowing enough. I continued in, and everyone but me saw I was still coming in way too fast. My crew chief told me again, "Sir, you need to slow down!" By that time, I was very close to the ground. I finally realized my plan to get in and get out fast was too aggressive. I was heading to a crash site instead of a landing zone.

I started slowing the aircraft, but it still was not enough. I tried to ease the aircraft onto the ground, but in reality, I really needed to make aggressive control inputs and perhaps even to make a go-around and try the landing again.

As I was about to crash the aircraft, I felt the collective flight control snatch out of my left hand and all available power was applied to arrest our rate of descent. It needed to happen, and I had failed to do it. Someone else helped me, presumably the other pilot. We would often help each other out on the flight controls if we got ourselves into trouble. The aircraft still hit the ground very hard, but not enough to break it or hurt anyone on board. The aircraft bounced across the objective and finally stopped at the front door of the HVT's house. Our customers got out and started their assault, and no bad guys came out shooting, either.

Our crew chief let us know everyone was out, and cleared me to take off again. As the aircraft climbed and joined other aircraft in formation, I looked over at the other pilot.

"Thanks for your help on the controls," I said. I remember him looking back at me in the green glow of the cockpit.

"I didn't help. I had my maps in my hands," he replied. I could see he still did. His hands were full. He was not the one who helped me.

No one in the aircraft helped me. God showed up and helped where I fell short. I believe God, or an angel of God, took over and prevented me from crashing the helicopter that night. You often hear that there are no atheists in foxholes, but I will tell you there are few in helicopters as well.

It was only about twenty years earlier that I was a tenth-grade high school dropout with no hope of having a meaningful job or life. How did I grow from being a high school dropout to flying some of the most sensitive missions for our nation in the best military helicopter unit in the world? How do you get to a place where God intervenes on your behalf in a miraculous way? Through the course of my military service, including nine combat deployments to Iraq and Afghanistan, I have experienced several near-death incidents but always managed to walk away without a scratch on my body. Why would God protect me?

This is the story of how my life turned around and of God's unending mercy, patience, and love.

Introduction

> *"'For I know the plans I have for you' declares the Lord,*
> *'plans to prosper you and not to harm you, plans to give*
> *you hope and a future.'"*
> —Jeremiah 29:11

I love Jeremiah 29:11 because it speaks to what God wants for us, and it shows God's heart for us. He wants us to have hope and a future. He wants us to live rich and fulfilled lives. The verse speaks truth into a world that is filled with lies. The lies oftentimes come directly from our circumstance, family, and the hardships we endure. The negative things in our lives try to shape us and our futures, and even define who we are. It doesn't have to be that way, though.

We cannot always control our circumstances in life or choose our families, or how people treat us. However, we can control how we react to people and what we learn from those circumstances and hardships. Due to the hardships I have experienced in life, I could possibly justify being angry. Everything I wrote about in this book is real and tangible, and gave me many reasons to be angry and point my finger at what others have done to me and the ones I love. I had legitimate reasons for dropping out of high school. If I were to live in a place of anger and resentment, though, it would steal whatever joy I have left. I decided to use these things as lessons for growth. God is sovereign even in times of difficulty.

In Genesis 37–41, Joseph had a lot of bad things happen to him. He was thrown into a pit to die, sold into slavery, put in jail, and left to rot in prison for a crime he did not commit. Joseph could have wallowed in his misery or lashed out at his brothers for starting the sequence of events. Instead, Joseph used what he learned through hardship to help his family and an entire nation. God did not cause bad things to happen to Joseph, but because of Joseph's attitude and obedience, God blessed Joseph and used him to do great things in spite of—or maybe because of—his troubles.

My life is a modern-day Joseph story but on a much smaller scale. I experienced abuse, worry, and turmoil throughout childhood. We lived in a state of survival. My biological father left us when I was an infant, and my stepdad, who I called Dad, was the only earthly father I knew, but he abused all of us, both physically and mentally. I spent my days living in fear. I daydreamed about a better day, a better way, and honestly just something *better*. I could not—or would not—focus in school. That led me to fail and repeat a couple grade levels. Eventually, I dropped out my sophomore year of high school. Then, I got my girlfriend pregnant. I worked as a construction laborer and could not provide for my new family. Eventually, I obtained my GED (General Equivalency Diploma), and that set my life on a better journey.

Today, my life is much better. I started my career in the infantry as an enlisted soldier. I was promoted to a Warrant Officer and later a Commissioned Officer. I eventually retired from the Army after more than two decades of service. While serving in the military, I continued my education. I received a Bachelor of Science in Aeronautics, a Master of Aeronautical Science, and a PhD in Public Policy. I am now a Master Instructor and Course Director for a military university and an adjunct professor for a traditional, non-military university.

I am the father of five wonderful boys who are well-adjusted and loved. I also have a wonderful wife who has partnered with me in our growing ministry. SEAKERS Aquatic Adventures is a 501(c)(3) nonprofit based in Concord, North Carolina. We use scuba diving to reach youth and at-risk youth, and to serve families, public servants, and people with disabilities. We also share the gospel with them and everyone we come in contact with. We started our work with at-risk youth because of my own life experiences.

So, how did I get from a high school drop-out and become a military pilot, obtain a PhD and start a nonprofit? I want to share the lessons I learned, and in some cases, relearned along the way. The lessons are timeless and may apply to your life as it did mine. My walk with Jesus Christ, however, had the biggest impact on my life. Through His grace and mercy, and in spite of my failings and upbringing, I was able to succeed when I should have failed.

This book is not just a story of how I got from GED to PhD, but all the stuff in the middle. There was no instant fix that helped me get from failure to relative success. I experienced a lot of messiness, and still do at times in my life. I continue to grow in my faith and as a man, father, husband, brother, son, and uncle.

If I was able to choose one situation that led to a positive change in my life, it would be my walk with God. If we can love God with all our hearts, souls, and minds, and love one another, the gates of hell cannot stand against us. No matter what we face in life, God and His love will not only triumph and prosper, but we will find our purpose. That purpose may come directly from the things we struggled with most in life. God uses bad moments in life to help us achieve goodness. Overcoming the bad is just as much your choice as it is God's desire. Start by choosing love, and then choosing better for you and others. To love God, though, you must also seek Him in all things: relationships, troubles, and the goodness in your life. Finally, gratitude is the underlying glue to all of this. Be grateful in both the good and bad things in life.

The first three life lessons I want to share with you are foundational. They are supported by scripture, which I believe is the main ingredient for a lesson to be truly life-changing. Scripture is the inspired Word of God. The Bible is our instruction manual here on Earth.

While I am the primary author of this book, Christina, who I call Wonder Woman, my lovely wife, assisted me in adding the Word of God.

Lesson One

Love God and each other above all else. God's greatest commandment to us is to love Him with all our hearts and souls, and then to love one another. This is foundational to all things good in life.

"Jesus replied, 'You must love the Lord your God with all your heart, all your soul, and all your mind. This is the first and greatest commandment. A second is equally important: Love your neighbor as yourself,'" (Matt. 22:37–39).

Lesson Two

In order to receive God's blessings and protections, you must seek Him. At the beginning of this passage I only listed Jerimiah 29:11. I included two more verses below because they are key. You must seek God, and He will hear you, and He will bless your life in more ways than you can imagine.

"'For I know the plans I have for you,' declares the Lord, 'plans to prosper you and not to harm you, plans to give you hope and a future. In those days when you pray, I will listen. If you look for me wholeheartedly, you will find me,'" (Jer. 29:11–13).

Lesson Three

Attitude is everything. More specifically, having an attitude of gratitude sets the tone for everything. Being thankful, even in moments of struggle, is critical to both your own joy and also your relationship with Christ. It's believing—truly believing—that God does all things for His purpose and your good. He cares, even about the smallest details of your life. If given the opportunity, He will bring good in all things, even situations that are difficult or horrible. Trust God in your bad times.

"Rejoice always, pray continually, give thanks in all circumstances; for this is God's will for you in Christ Jesus" (1 Thes. 5:16–18).

Chapter 1

Be Present

"Only a life lived for others is a life worthwhile."
—Albert Einstein

It would be an understatement to say I had a hard childhood. My mother has always been very loving and tended to make poor decisions about husbands until she married her current husband. My biological father left before I had any memory of him. He was not in our lives until my siblings and I became adults.

My mother's second husband was not all bad. In fact, he could be a lot of fun at times. Early on, however, he was mostly mean and selfish. In full disclosure, I have made peace with him and do not harbor bad feelings toward him. He is a significant part of my story, and one I suspect many readers can relate to.

We lived in Miami Shores, Florida. My mother previously moved there from Buffalo, New York, to be near my grandparents—the heroes of my life. My grandparents, Jim and Helen Bowen, were my safe place throughout my childhood. They lived in Hialeah, Florida, which was nearby. My grandparents were not rich, famous, or notable for doing anything monumental, but they were significant to me. Grandad was a US postal worker, and Gammy worked for Sears. They worked hard, saved, and spent their money wisely, and were my only example of normal. My grandparents have always been my inspiration.

My mother struggles with decisions she made that negatively affected my siblings and me, but her decision to be near my grandparents was a gift she may not realize she gave us.

Regular people can be heroes, too. If you are present, available, and loving, you can have a significant impact on people. Second only to God's grace and blessings, I contribute any accomplishments I have had in life to my grandparents. They were present and that was enough.

Lesson Four

Be present. You never know the impact you can have on someone. You could change someone's life, and you may never know it. Be present with the people you love and show them what *right* looks like.

"Be completely humble and gentle; be patient, bearing with one another in love. Make every effort to keep the unity of the Spirit through the bond of peace" (Eph. 4:2–3).

Chapter 2

Predictions

"You can't let your past hold your future hostage."
—LL Cool J

I devoted this space in my book to my dad. For better or worse, he had significant impact on me as a child. The word *impact* has more than one meaning here, too. Over time, he has changed for the better, at least as far as my relationship with him goes. He is much easier to get along with now. I am not sure if that's because he is older now or because I now have a choice or because he suffered a life-changing stroke in 1995. Whatever the cause, our relationship is better these days. To be fair, he was there when my biological father was not. I think he struggled with the idea that he was not our biological father but our stepdad. Growing up, we went by his last name instead of McAteer—our legal name—until he and my mom divorced when I was about twelve years old.

This is not to shame my dad or speak bad of him. It's merely part of my story and who I have become. I need to say this for context if nothing else: He, like the rest of us, comes from a broken place.

Also, to be fair to my dad, in many ways my childhood was a reflection of his childhood. His dad was probably meaner than he was. My dad experienced a difficult childhood, too. I'd like to share another lesson: Your past does not have to determine who you become, but it *can* if you let it.

3

We often inherit the sins of our families, which are called generational sins. These sins are a pattern we can continue in our own lives if we are not careful, and we can pass on to our children. The same sins can last for generations if we don't break the cycle.

I think my dad continued behavior he saw in his own home. I'm not making an excuse for his actions; we all have free will, but our pasts can serve as a road map for our future. It takes deliberate determination to change course and do better. I am not a perfect dad to my five boys by any stretch of the imagination, but I chose to be different than my father. Instead of looking back on my past and seeing it for only the negatives, I drew on those experiences to make a positive change and to be better.

Lesson Five

Your past does not have to predict your future, but it can if you let it. It can also predict the future for those you love in both positive and negative ways. Your negative life lessons provide an opportunity for change. Generational sins must be broken, or they will continue. The only way to break the cycle is through a personal relationship with Jesus Christ. He is the breaker of the chains that bind and define us.

"See, I am doing a new thing! Now it springs up; do you not perceive it? I am making a way in the wilderness and streams in the wasteland" (Isa. 43:19).

Chapter 3

Forgiveness

"Forgiveness does not mean excusing."
—C.S. Lewis

My earliest memory was when I was about four years old. We were living in Miami Shores. My dad, a Vietnam veteran, was probably experiencing post-traumatic stress disorder (PTSD). Maybe that explains why he was so abusive, or maybe it was the alcohol or both. Maybe he was just mean; I don't know. Life was not easy for my mom or my siblings and me.

I was the youngest of three until my little sister, Jaime, came along later. Nadara is my older sister, and Craig is my older brother. Our house was a place of constant fear and worry. We were fearful when my dad was home, and when he was gone, we worried about what would happen when he got home. We didn't know which version of him would show up. Would he be mean Dad or fun Dad? In hindsight, I think we got a version of him proportional to the amount of alcohol he consumed and how his day went. The entire time we lived under his roof, we would always scatter like mice when he got home. Often, we would be watching TV and would see his headlights flash across the living room walls. We would scatter and wait.

If nice Dad came home, he would eat dinner in front of the TV. By the time we came to the conclusion the nice version of him was home, we would creep into the living room and watch whatever he had on. We tried not to be noticed or change the mood. We would watch *The Smothers Brothers, Sonny and Cher, The Mandrel Sisters, The Six Million Dollar Man,* and *Chopper 1.* Watching TV as a family was often the calmest and, therefore, happiest times at home. Even fun Dad was not always fun for us. We would start out watching TV, and then my dad would pull out his BB gun. He was not angry but just wanted to have a little fun—at our expense.

We would be given a couple of seconds to run down the hall and hide. Then, Dad started shooting. We always got shot; there was no getting away. Even when we made it to our rooms, and out of direct fire, he was able to ricochet BBs off the wall and still hit us.

Later, when we were a bit older, Dad hunted us down in the woods and shot us when he found us. The crazy thing is, as much as we didn't like getting shot, it was better than angry Dad. I remember forcing a smile when he found me because he was typically in a great mood when this was going on, so we would play along. To be clear, the "game" was never fun and taught us all a bad behavior that Craig and I carried through our teenage years.

As BB guns became more powerful, Craig and I hunted and shot each other, and we both ended up in the hospital—a doctor digging for BBs or cutting them out. I once shot Craig in the head, and a doctor had to remove the BB from Craig's scalp. Another time, I shot him in the bridge of the nose, almost hitting him in the eye. It's amazing none of us were seriously injured.

One time, Dad gave Craig the gun and told him he could take a shot at him as he ran down the hall to the bathroom for a shower. Dad said Craig would not get in trouble if he was successful. We were so young, and Dad knew Craig would not get the gun cocked in time. It was too difficult for him. It was one of Dad's rare miscalculations. As Dad ran down the hall, he made it to the bathroom for his shower. As expected, Craig could not cock the gun before Dad made it to the bathroom. Between the two of us, however, we got the gun cocked. Dad tried to be cute, sticking his bare rear end out the bathroom door. Craig had an accurate aim and hit Dad in his bare backside. Because it was fun Dad, Craig did not get a beating.

Even when our dad "played" with us, it was rough, and we did not enjoy it. When he made a joke, we would all laugh whether the joke was funny or not, or if we did not understand the joke. Most of his jokes were racial slurs or fat shaming, or he made jokes about us. It was more like he picked on us for something we did or how we looked or something. And that's the way it was in our house. Someone would be the target of harassment for the day, and everyone else was glad they weren't in the crosshairs of Dad's jokes.

Mean Dad was a completely different experience. It was not hard to discern, either. While we hid in our rooms, we would hear the yelling start. Sometimes he yelled because his dinner was cold or because he didn't like something or because the house was not quite right. It really came down to his mood more than anything, but someone would pay the price for his mood. Often, my mom, Elaine, took a lot of abuse from Dad. My siblings and I heard the yelling from our hiding spots, hoping we would not become the next victim. At some point, we would be called out, either one-by-one or as a group.

We never knew what we would get in trouble for, but there would be something we did or did not do. We learned very early on that it was better to confess to something we did not do and get the beating than to defend our honor. I am still sensitive to this with my own children and often find myself giving them the benefit of doubt instead of forcing a confession that may or may not be true.

My dad's beatings were not nice or gentle. He often used a leather belt, an open hand, and sometimes, as we got older, a closed hand. Mostly, he used a belt because it left marks—big, ugly marks. During the summer months, my siblings and I wore long pants a lot to cover the black-and-blue marks. The beatings were brutal, but they were pretty normal to us because of the frequency we received them.

Craig and I were forced to fist fight each other or take a beating from Dad, or sometimes both. I can remember looking at my big brother and him looking back at me; neither of us wanted to hit the other, but we eventually did because Dad's beating would be worse. If we took it easy on each other, like we often tried to do, Dad noticed, and we were either forced to fight harder or we had to fight Dad. We would fight harder, but in the end we often had to fight Dad, too. We were never successful when we fought Dad; we were just little boys, and he was an adult.

When I mentioned that my relationship is better with my dad now, I meant it. I forgave him for things that took place when I was a child. I carried my anger around for years, but I learned it was not helpful or beneficial to my life. I learned that unconditional forgiveness was actually the way to a better future for myself and those around me. Carrying around my anger kept me from realizing my full potential and negatively affected my future. More importantly, since God forgave me, I also need to forgive others, even when it's difficult.

Lesson Six

Unconditional forgiveness is the key to having an abundant and joyful life. Forgiveness is more for the person who forgives than for the person receiving forgiveness. Carrying around anger and resentment has a way of stealing the joy from your life. Forgive and move on. It may take conscious effort or even years of reaffirming your forgiveness, but eventually your heart will follow. Not forgiving others can lead to hate, anger, jealousy, and even feeling physically sick. A lack of forgiveness can also steal from other relationships, and leave you empty and joyless. Our other relationships suffer as we carry around anger, resentment, and unresolved issues.

Ephesians 4:31–32 states, "Get rid of all bitterness, rage and anger, brawling and slander, along with every form of malice. Be kind and compassionate to one another, forgiving each other, just as in Christ God forgave you."

I learned other lessons from life with my dad, including resilience, and how not to be as a parent. This might seem obvious, but many parents carry over examples they learned as a child to their own children. Some never recognize they're using the wrong set of parenting tips.

Chapter 4

Irrational Fear

> *"Fear is a liar."*
> —Zach Williams

My mother holds a lot of guilt about our early life experiences. She feels guilty that she didn't do enough to protect us. I think she tried her best; she has always been loving, but she was not equipped to deal with our dad. She was very young when she got married. We all tried to survive on a day-to-day basis, and I don't blame her for my dad's actions. She was scared. She was just as scared, which was probably rational fear to a point, as we were. But she was also afraid of the unknown and not being able to provide for her family.

My mom was born in Staten Island, New York, and I think she had a pretty normal childhood. Her brother and sister were half-blood siblings, and both were significantly older than her. Her brother was born during her father's previous marriage, and her sister was born during her mom's previous marriage. Because of the age difference, my mom was the only child in the house.

My mother married and divorced her first husband, my biological father, in Buffalo, New York and later married my dad after moving from Buffalo to Miami. Before they got married, my mom, my siblings, and I lived with my grandparents until we moved into a house in Miami Shores. From there, we moved around a lot before finally settling in Summerville, South Carolina, which is a small town near Charleston.

My mom was the moral compass for us. She was our source of inspiration. She taught us about Jesus Christ and regularly took us to church. That early exposure to church and faith has carried me throughout life and now shapes the ministry I lead.

Dad wasn't just abusive to us kids and my mother, he cheated on her multiple times as well. He drank a lot, and provided very little money for us to live on. My parents were always behind on rent, which led to us moving around a lot. My mom left my dad on more than one occasion, but she always went back. Sometimes it was because he stalked her. Other times, it was because she felt like she did not have any other choice. When I was about twelve years old, she left for the last time and got a divorce. That started a new chapter for all of us. It posed its own set of challenges, but at least my mother finally overcame her fear of leaving my dad.

In the context of God's design, fear is a good and powerful thing. It often manifests in fight or flight situations. If we find ourselves in mortal danger, we have to make a quick decision and act. Imagine if a wild animal attacked you, your fight or flight response could save your life.

I experienced a lot of fear while on the battlefield. The first time I went to Iraq, as part of 1st Armored Division's 6/6 Infantry during Operation Desert Storm, we were going in to fight our first major battle in Al Busayya. The fear gripped me as we moved the Bradley Fighting Vehicles and M1 Abrams tanks toward the town and began firing. The fear I felt in those moments was real and necessary fear. It was rational fear, which creates the release of adrenalin and increases oxygen flow to our muscles. Those bodily reactions help us focus.

But there is another fear that is not of God's design. It relates to worry, inaction, or the wrong action. Irrational fear can lead to poor physical and mental health, such as stomach ulcers and depression.

This type of fear stems from fear of failure, growing old, fear of judgment or humiliation, or fear of not being able to care for yourself or your loved ones. These are irrational fears because if we put our faith in God, we could overcome those fears. My mother has had irrational fears most of her life, and certainly had them when my siblings and I were young. Her fear kept her in a marriage that was physically and mentally abusive.

Fear distracts us from God's promises and holds us in bondage. Fear is a liar. Not only can it steal your joy, but it can also prevent God's planned goodness for your life. God loves you and wants you to have hope, joy, and a good life. You must choose to let go of fear and trust Him to handle the unknowns in your life in order to receive His blessings. My mother was and is a godly woman, but she lived in fear and did not turn her worries over to God. We were not created to live in perpetual places of fear.

Lesson Seven

We do not need to fear anything when we allow God to be in control of our lives. He will provide for our needs and protect us.

"For God has not given us a spirit of fear, but of power and of love and of a sound mind" (2 Tim. 1:7).

"And we know that God causes everything to work together for the good of those who love God, and are called according to his purpose for them" (Rom. 8:28).

Chapter 5

How Many Times Do You Forgive?

"Peter came to the Lord and asked, 'Lord, how many times shall I forgive someone who has done something wrong to me? Is seven times enough?'"
—Matthew 18:21

This book is the first time I have openly talked about my child-hood. It has been a source of shame within my family. I don't talk about it with my children, though I expect I will now. I mentioned earlier that my biological father left us when I was an infant. No one was sure where he went or why he left his family to fend for themselves. It takes a special kind of evil to abandon your family, particularly since we know more about him and his ways now—he is a very evil person.

I always wondered about my biological father and why he left. I thought more about it as I got older, and my mom was willing to discuss it and speculate, but she didn't know, either. She did say my biological father would most likely avoid being found, at least until we were eighteen, so he would not have to pay child support. His Social Security number and name is all I had.

I decided to look for him in 1996 when I was twenty-seven and a divorced father of three. I wanted to know more about him. Was he the same person? Had he changed? Had something happened in his life that forced him to act the way he did? I wanted to find out. My need for answers about my biological dad created a strain between my dad and me. By that point, Dad and I got along well, but we did not communicate regularly. So, I didn't tell him what I was doing. At some point, though, someone must have told him. I am not sure if that hurt him or not, but I hope it didn't.

I wrote a letter to my biological father, telling him a little about myself and that I was interested in meeting him. I sent this letter to the IRS with his name and Social Security number and asked if they would forward it to him. I wasn't sure if they would do it or not, and, to be honest, I sort of forgot about it.

One day, I got a letter from my biological father. He wanted to meet my siblings and me. I called my brother and sister and my mother, to tell them. My siblings were both interested in meeting him as well. I had been selected for Officer Candidate School and needed to report to Ft. Benning, so I planned to meet with my biological father then because it was near his home.

During the visit, my father was engaged and interested in my life, and we agreed to stay in touch and continue our relationship. At some point, my brother and sister met with him as well. For the next few years, we continued to pop in and out of each other's lives. He disappeared at one point, only to resurface again. I found out he had another family he also bailed on. So, I have at least three half siblings I have never met.

My father was not honest about much. He claimed to have stomach cancer, and there always seemed to be something going on with him that demanded sympathy from others. Those situations always turned out to be lies. Given his past, however, none of us siblings were surprised, so I humored him and didn't make a big deal about his lying. I decided any relationship was better than none, so I looked past the warning signs. He was my biological father after all, and I made the effort to forgive him over and over again.

My father was an avid scuba diver—something I had always wanted to do—and he eventually attended a scuba instructor course in the Florida Keys. At the time, he was remarried, and it was not going well. So, my father ditched his wife and moved to Key Largo to live on a boat and become a scuba instructor. My friends and I would visit him; the Keys might be my favorite place in the world. My father certified me as a scuba diver but did not do a very good job at all. I learned the most basic scuba lessons on my own and eventually took *real,* advanced scuba courses, and my skills improved. I don't think my father ever even got in the water with me when I got certified. Instead, he turned me loose in the marina and watched from a dock. Not surprisingly, he always took the easy way out.

While I was in the Army, I moved around a lot: Savannah, Georgia; Roosevelt Roads, Puerto Rico; Ft. Rucker, Alabama; and so on. My father visited, and I went to see him. That pattern continued for some years. He eventually moved in with one of my sisters in South Carolina Knowing what I know now, I think he ran from something back in Florida, but I am not entirely sure. I do know he was not working as a computer programmer anymore and instead worked as a clerk in a gas station. He was down on his luck. I had a conversation with him, and I asked him where God was in his life. He said he and God had an understanding, and he was not interested in what God had to say. I thought things would not go well, and they did not.

I was stationed in Savannah, Georgia when I got a call one morning in 2002. My biological father had been arrested for molesting one of my nieces. I was devastated. I was responsible for bringing him back into all our lives.

My father went to jail and was convicted. He is now out of jail after serving several years, and I have not heard from him. He had the nerve to write my sister and ask for money—the same sister whose daughter he molested. I have forgiven my father once again, but I don't want a relationship with him anymore. His reign of terror is over.

Lesson Eight

How many times do you forgive someone? As many as it takes, but you may want to limit your exposure at some point. My biological father did some horrible things to us, but we are commanded to forgive because we are forgiven. By forgiving him, I don't carry hate around with me, but I also have chosen not to expose myself to him and his behavior anymore.

"If you forgive those who sin against you, your Heavenly Father will forgive you" (Matt. 6:14).

Lesson Nine

Forgiving someone does not mean you have to have a relationship with them; it means you let go of past hurts. You remember without anger. So many people struggle with forgiveness because they don't fully understand what it means or what it *can* mean. When you forgive someone, you forgive a hurt or action. You are not expecting that everything go back the way it was. I also learned that I probably should have decided to end the relationship with my father long ago, and I could have prevented more hurt in my life. Either way, though, I chose to forgive him.

"Then Peter came to Jesus and asked, 'Lord, how many times shall I forgive my brother or sister who sins against me? Up to seven times?' Jesus answered, 'I tell you, not seven times, but seventy-seven times'" (Matt. 18:21–22).

Chapter 6

Is Church or Organized Christian Fellowship Necessary?

"Wherever we see the Word of God purely preached and heard, there a church of God exists, even if it swarms with many faults."
—John Calvin

I use the ugliness of my childhood for good, which is just as God intended. My faith is the greatest gift my mother gave me. God has had the best and most significant impact on who I am. My mother taught us about God's love and always took us to church, even when our home life was tumultuous. Church was a refuge. God's message planted the seeds. Some of you may wonder where God was during the worst times at home, but I know He was there with us.

We all have free will and the ability to choose between good and evil. What is the point of life without free will? If we have no freedom to make our own choices, then we are nothing more than robots. More importantly, we are meant to love, and we cannot choose love without free will and choosing love, even when difficult to do so, underscores what it means to be a Christian. Some of us make godly decisions that shape our actions, and others make poor decisions. The truth is, we all do both throughout our lives.

Many people call Christians hypocrites because of this, but it is our sinful nature, the struggle between right and wrong. It is not hypocritical to fail on occasion; it's human nature. We all fall short and sin. Being a Christian is not a destination; it's the journey of learning and building a relationship with Christ. Being a Christian is a journey of growth and learning to be more like Him.

I have not always been faithful to God. I had a relationship with Jesus Christ that ebbed and flowed depending on where I was in life. Like most friendships, if you don't surround yourself with people who have the same morals as you, you can drift away from what is most important. God, however, is always steadfast.

This leads me to my next life lesson: you must surround yourself with godly people and go to church more. When I was a teenager and drifted from God, I often said, "You don't have to go to church to be saved or to go to heaven." While that is true, that mind-set can be damaging and deceptive.

Church attendance is not what gets us into heaven, but the relationships we develop at church will enrich our lives. When I did not attend some sort of church service, I drifted from my relationship with God. That relationship, however, is the most meaningful part. Being a Christian is not about going to church or being religious. It is about the relationship with Christ that opens your heart to the Holy Spirit.

God's goal is to have a relationship with you. We ask about our purposes. One of our purposes is to have a life-changing, real relationship with God, and everything else will follow. What should we be doing with our lives? What jobs should we have? How should we raise our children? What is our purpose on Earth? If we spent more time following God and less time worrying about our purpose, we'd be able to accomplish it all. All these things will become self-evident after the relationship is built. We start to allow God to lead as opposed to being driven by our own desires because we start hearing the Holy Spirit. We can't hear the Holy Spirit through all of life's noises if we don't have a relationship with Him first. We need to stop worrying about our purposes and more about our relationship with God. Then our purposes will follow.

In order to understand what it is to be a Christian and reap the full benefits of our faith, we must understand God and His heart for us. We get that by immersing ourselves in learning about Him through sermons, biblical classes, and small group discussions. If we want to be proficient at anything in life, such as our jobs, we have to go to college or trade school. The same is true about learning about Christ.

Lesson Ten

Regularly attending church is important for your development and growth as a Christian. Many people view Christianity as legalistic, such as following the Ten Commandments. But it's much more than that. Christianity is about finding the purpose God has for you and building a relationship with Him. We are meant to live in community with one another, lifting each other up, and giving hope. Here are some other reasons to attend church or participate in Christian fellowship:

God commands it. Hebrews 10:25 states, "And let us not neglect our meeting together, as some people do, but encourage one another, especially now that the day of his return is drawing near."

We are meant to live in community.

It is essential for spiritual growth. We are influenced by the company we keep and being around strong believers helps us in our own journey and faith.

"Jesus said, 'Where two or three are gathered in my name, there am I among them'" (Matt. 18:20). Worshiping Jesus in numbers is extremely powerful; He promises to be among us.

Because it reminds us of who we are in Christ.

It's the only consistent way most of us can worship God and learn more about Him and His Word.

It gives you a consistent place to serve others.

It helps you overcome the eight-inch barrier. There are about eight inches that separate your head and heart. Many people, who don't go to church, understand our faith in their head, but the lack of worship opportunities and relationships prevent their faith from moving to their hearts, which is where the most significant things happen as a believer in Christ.

Lesson Eleven

Christians are not perfect. I often hear people say Christians are hypocrites because they do things the Bible tells us not to do. My previous pastor in Savannah, Georgia, used to say that if we put our faith in him, he will disappoint us one day — not because he wants to but because he is human and will let people down. We all fall short of God's commandments. Our goal is not to sin, but we all do, and that does not make Christians hypocrites; it makes us human. Having said that, we should repent and end patterns of sin.

"Indeed, there is not a righteous man on earth who continually does good and who never sins" (Eccles. 7:20).

Lesson Twelve

Serving others helps you more than it helps the people you serve. I often heard from people who went on mission trips that they got more out of the trip than the people they helped. I never understood that until I took my first short-term mission trip. I was filled with hope, joy, and appreciation during my trip and when I returned home. There is something about helping others that gives us a sense of purpose, love, and hope. The same thing happens when we serve our communities or our families. Relationships are born, and purpose is given. While church attendance is not the only way to serve others, it does provide a lot of opportunity to do so. For Christians, it also allows us to serve in the context of Christ and even provides opportunities to share the gospel.

"You, my brothers and sisters, were called to be free. But do not use your freedom to indulge in the flesh; rather, serve one another humbly in love" (Gal. 5:13).

Invitation

I would like to take this opportunity to invite you to church. My invitation is good at any Christian church near you, and I can confidently say you will be welcomed with open arms. If you happen to live in the Greater Charlotte area, I would like to invite you to Crossroads Church in Concord, North Carolina. Our senior pastor, Lowell McNaney, and the Crossroads staff are anointed and love to share the good news. That church is where my wife, Christina, and I have grown in faith, love, and hope. It is a place we have served and been served for several years. It is also where we started our nonprofit, SEAKERS. Other great ministries, such as CAPSTONE Climbing Adventures, which is led by Lenny Stallings was started there as well. I say that because it's a unique church that produces people who love God and serve others.

This church is only one of thousands of Christian churches spread throughout this country and world. So, if the first church you try is not a good fit, try another. There is a church for everyone. Some people need formality. Some like old-time hymns, and others like a more contemporary feel. So, find the one you're comfortable in that also teaches God's Word.

Lesson Thirteen

Invite someone to church. An invitation to church can be life-saving for someone, and the ripple effects from that simple invitation can be significant.

"Go therefore and make disciples of all nations, baptizing them in the name of the Father and of the Son and of the Holy Spirit, teaching them to observe all that I have commanded you. And behold, I am with you always, to the end of the age" (Matt. 28:19–20).

Chapter 7

God Wants You to Dream

"A man is not old until regrets take the place of dreams."
—John Barrymore

After dropping out of high school, I worked in a grocery store and then the construction industry. Neither, however, were my dream jobs. I didn't have any dreams for my life, though. If I had any at all, they were abandoned many years before I dropped out of school. I merely existed. I had no idea where I was going or where I came from. I had no identity, no hope, and no dreams. I subconsciously accepted my place in the world. After working for a few years, though, I found myself wanting something different. Through books, I rediscovered a dream I had growing up. I wanted to join the Army or the Navy and get into special operations. I had a problem, though. I didn't have the required high school diploma. So, I decided to get my General Equivalency Diploma (GED). Some branches of the military accepted a GED.

I wanted to be a Navy SEAL, but with a poor track record up to that point in my life, I decided it was too risky. If I failed out of SEAL training, I could've ended up cleaning toilets on a ship. I elected to join the Army instead. And I ended up cleaning a lot of toilets anyway! Actually, I joined the South Carolina Army National Guard because the Guard was one of the only branches that accepted a GED. Craig joined a few years earlier. Growing up, we both shared the desire to be infantrymen, which created an avenue to special operations. Craig went to basic training and advanced infantry training and brought back stories of adventure and shooting real M16s. So, I decided the National Guard was the outfit for me.

My brother got assigned to the Summerville, South Carolina, Infantry unit, and I went to Monk's Corner, South Carolina, Infantry unit.

In 1986, I went to basic training in Ft. Benning, Georgia, and that experience was pure shock to my system. Basic training was not kinder and gentler like it is today. Basic training was sink or swim from day one. I was not the fittest of trainees, but I was in desperate need of discipline, fitness, and meaning. The Army gave that to me. It was a defining moment for me, and my only regret was that I had to join the Guard instead of active duty Army. After basic and advanced infantry school, I had to go home to my old job. I was a weekend warrior. The Guard is different now, but in those days, it was not very serious. Most people just wanted the paycheck and did not care about training or being a soldier.

My first day of basic training was full of yelling, pushups, running, and indoctrination. It was pretty unnerving for most of us. One person in my platoon asked to go to the bathroom during an indoctrination session. We learned then that the Army does not have bathrooms. His request was denied. A short time later, a yellow puddle formed around the feet of the same recruit and ran down to the drill sergeant's feet. We learned what mass punishment was that day. We all paid for that error with pushups and six-inch leg lifts right there in the pee. By the way, the Army has latrines, not bathrooms.

I began to excel in basic training. My childhood taught me to follow orders to the T. That's what the Army wanted during training. I became very good at shooting, marching, and soldiering in general. At one range, we had to crawl under concertina (razor) wire while real machine guns fired over our heads. Explosions went off all around us, and some guys froze with fear. I, however, thrived and loved it. I started to identify myself with something positive for the first time in my life. At the last comprehensive infantry test, I received a perfect score on all my skills—only a few in the entire company earned the plaque that came with it. I was really proud to be a solider and an infantryman.

Lesson Fourteen

God wants you to dream about a better day and a better way, but in the context of His purpose. Some dreams come from God if you let them. The Holy Spirit inspires and guides you—if you let it.

"Joshua said to them, 'Do not be afraid; do not be discouraged. Be strong and courageous. This is what the LORD will do to all the enemies you are going to fight'" (Josh. 10:25).

Chapter 8

Your Purpose Can Still Be Fulfilled in an Unfulfilling Job

"The best way to appreciate your job is to imagine yourself without one."
—Oscar Wilde

I went home to South Carolina once I graduated basic training. I had to go back to my job in the construction field. I did pretty well. I had a decent job and also received a paycheck from the National Guard. So, I decided to buy a new truck. I purchased a 1987 Ford Ranger. I went over to my boss's house the day I bought it. I wanted to show it to him. I locked the keys in the cab while it was running. I could not break into it, so I had to cut the back window rubber gasket to get inside. I was devastated that my new truck was already broken.

My first experiences in my local National Guard were disappointing. I saw myself as a steely-eyed killer after graduating basic training, but no one in my unit shared the desire to be a warrior. All they wanted to do was put in a weekend and annual training each year for a paycheck. No one really wanted to be there. Wearing the uniform and being there still gave me some direction and purpose.

In 1987, during my first *real* post-basic training exercise included two weeks of training at Ft. Stewart in Georgia. No one else seemed interested in being there, but I was. My unit was a mechanized infantry unit with an M113 Armored Personnel Carrier. We did normal maneuvers that were interesting, but the defining moment for me was catching a small spotted deer. I snuck up and caught a spotted dear that had lost its mother. I know I'll probably catch it from the environmentalists, but it was a long time ago and I was very young. I felt cool at the time. In fact, I became a warrior of sorts in my unit. My company commander caught wind of it and posed with the deer himself. It was as if I was meant to catch that deer.

A short time later, my commander changed command and transferred to battalion in Mt. Pleasant, South Carolina. He had to put together a new Long-Range Reconnaissance Patrol (LRRP) Team. Under normal circumstances, I would not have had a chance to get into that specialized unit, but my commander remembered the deer and he requested me before the LRRP team selection board. I don't remember much about the interview, but they all wanted to hear about the deer I caught. I was selected for the team and reassigned. Because of the deer, I was designated as a survival specialist. I took my duty seriously. I memorized the Army Field Manual (FM) 21–76, US Army Survival Manual.

At the next annual training, my unit did a lot of interesting work. During one mission, we flew in a UH-1 Huey helicopter, dropped off behind the enemy, and were given targets and enemy positions to look for. On one patrol, I was number three in a three-man team. The lead guy never saw the Eastern Diamond Back rattler. The second guy jumped over it. And I stopped as soon as I saw it, which was too late. It was within striking distance and quickly tried to bite me. The snake was a juvenile, and its fangs did not penetrate my combat boot. I pinned the snake down with my M16, then cut off its head and stuck the snake in one of my cargo pockets. I ate a rattlesnake as a kid, so I thought I could cook him for the team that night. That also fulfilled my duties as the team survival specialist.

We continued on patrol until we reached the main patrol base. We were sent to recon an enemy-held bridge. As we got closer, the team split up, and we each went to a separate position to get different perspectives.

I had to go through a swamp area. As I walked, I looked down and saw I had stepped next to another snake. It faced away from me but quickly turned. It recognized it was a water moccasin. I adeptly pinned its upper body underwater before it could bite me. I didn't know exactly where the snake's head was, so it took me a minute to muster up the courage to put my hand in the water and find its head. I needed to pick the snake up without getting bit. The snake was a bit bigger than the rattler, but after I cut off its head, the snake still fit in my other cargo pocket. After that mission, we went back to base. I took both snakes out of my pockets and tossed them in the middle of the team. Everyone scattered like mice. It was pretty funny for me, but the other guys scolded me for doing it. Even so, it helped my reputation with the team and the unit. I had one deer and two snakes to my credit.

Sometime later, a local Junior Reserve Officer Training Corps (JROTC) unit requested my unit deliver a survival class while they were bivouacking (military for camping). Since I was the unit's subject matter expert (SME) on survival, I was asked to do the class. I jumped at the chance. I had a month to prepare for the class.

A friend of mine captured an opossum in his rabbit trap and did not know what to do with it, but I did. I took it off his hands and used it for my survival class. If it wasn't for opossum and dandelions, many people would have starved during the Depression. I kept the opossum in a cage and fed it clean food for a few weeks. Opossum's are not famous for clean diets and will pretty much eat whatever they come across. Every time I saw the opossum in its cage, it was very still. I didn't consider the fact that they were nocturnal and were famous for "playing possum."

I asked Craig to assist with the class because he was still in the guard. He happily agreed. On the day of the class, I went to the cage and foolishly grabbed this opossum by the scruff of the neck and threw him in back of my pickup truck. It was not very active, and I thought it would stay put. We planned to take the opossum out of the neighborhood and shoot it with a .22 caliber rifle I had. Then we would go to the JROTC site.

A little way down the road, Craig turned around to check on the opossum. He started stuttering (he did not have a stuttering problem), clearly trying to tell me something important, but could not get the words out. Finally, he yelled, "The opossum is getting away!"

I looked in my driver's side mirror and saw the opossum leap from the side of my truck. My class project was on the loose. I had a pistol CO_2 powered BB gun in the truck. We both chased the opossum. We ended up cornering it in someone's yard. I shot it a couple of times to kill it. I put the opossum in the back of my truck again, with a renewed confidence that it would stay put. I know animal lovers will want to scold me, but I was young.

We arrived at the campsite and met the JROTC Commander, a major with about twenty-five high school students. I wanted to get the group's attention by starting with the opossum and then moving into survival academics. The opossum was dead, so I skinned it to cook over the fire. In doing so, I noticed small pink things attached to the stomach area, so I scraped four to six of them off. It finally occurred to me that those little pink things were opossum babies that were nursing. It had not even occurred to me that the opossum was a marsupial and that *he* was a *she!* Unfortunately, everyone watching knew exactly what I had done. When I looked up, everyone was staring at me like I was some kind of baby killer. I thought quickly and said, "These are bite size. You just pop them in your mouth." That broke the tension, and I explained I was unaware the opossum had babies.

I went on to finish cleaning the opossum and put it over the fire to cook while I finished the class. To my surprise, all the kids tried the cooked opossum. One of them asked me if I was going to have any. "Opossum will keep you alive, but it tastes terrible," I replied.

Lesson Fifteen

Sometimes you have to work a job that may not meet your expectations before you can earn a better position. Starting from the bottom is not all bad, and God often has some things for you to do to prepare you for the next and bigger thing. Like my friend, Pastor Lowell, from Crossroads Church says, "Sometimes God makes things happen now, but most of the time He brings you through a process because there is something you need to learn."

"Commit to the Lord in whatever you do, and He will establish your plans" (Prov. 16:3).

Chapter 9

God Is Sovereign Even in Your Bad Decisions

"Difficulties break some men but make others. No axe is sharp enough to cut the soul of a sinner who keeps on trying, one armed with the hope that he will rise even in the end."
—Nelson Mandela

While serving in the National Guard, I got an apartment with my childhood best friend, Mike. That was another bad decision. Mike changed while I was in Army basic training. He played in a heavy metal band, partied, and started doing drugs. Although I tried to fit in a little, I had changed, too. The lifestyle did not fit in with my new life as a soldier. I started dating Mike's younger sister, which had bittersweet consequences. I don't think Mike necessarily cared that I dated his sister, but things started falling apart, and Mike and I no longer got along. I unexpectedly came home to find Mike and his friends destroying our apartment. The rental agreement was in my name only. They trashed the apartment, putting holes in the wall. I called the police, but before they could arrive, Mike was off to join the Army and never really had to answer for it. I was so disappointed that Mike would do such a thing. While Mike never apologized for that, I chose to forgive him anyway.

I continued to date Mike's sister, and she ended up getting pregnant with my child. I continued making bad choices. I love my son, Marc, but life quickly became more complicated with a child.

We got married because she was pregnant. Life continued to get more difficult. Neither she nor I completed high school, which further contributed to our problems. We didn't even love each other, but we were having a child. After we got married, we moved in with my mom. Then we later moved in with Craig. Everyone was very generous with us; it just was not working out. We could not afford to get our own place, so I found a way to get on active duty in the Army. That turned out to be a great decision.

While waiting to go on active duty, I had the opportunity to go to Ft. Lewis, Washington, on active duty with the National Guard. It was a tough decision to go because Marc was due the same month I had to report, but we needed the money. To be honest, I was scared to death to be a father. I never had a good example of what a father could be. So, I went to Ft. Lewis. I think that angered my wife, and I can totally understand why a young woman would be angry about going through labor by herself. In hindsight, I should not have gone, even with the money problems. I was still making bad and selfish choices.

Ft. Lewis was interesting. Due to my LRRP background, I was assigned to a motorized scout platoon. We deployed to the field in South Rainier on a training exercise. I was assigned to be a .50 caliber machine gunner on a HMMWV (Hummer). My animal exploits finally caught up with me. While traveling down the road, we saw a small pack of coyotes cross the road in front of us. I had the vehicle stop, and I tracked them. I know what you're thinking: Why in the world would I do that? All I can say is, I was eighteen years old and a high school dropout. So, I was not very smart. I tracked one of the smaller coyotes into a thick brush and cornered it. The coyote was a juvenile, which probably helped. It was cornered, and I was quick enough to grab him by the scruff of the neck.

So, what does a young soldier do with a newly captured coyote? Well, he tries to feed it ham slices from Meals Ready to Eat (MRE). I relaxed my attention for a little too long, and the coyote turned and bit my left hand—enough to draw blood. That was not part of the plan. I tied the coyote to a tree stump while I considered my options. When I was not paying attention, the unit medic saw the animal and released it. I told the medic, who was new to the unit, that the coyote bit me. We discussed what we should do.

The medic wanted to report it higher up, but I did not. I rationalized to him that the animal looked healthy (it did not), and I was willing to risk the consequences, and that we should keep the incident between us. He agreed and we went our separate ways.

During the evening meal, my platoon sergeant shouted, "Specialist (SP4) McAteer, get your ass over here!"

I did.

"Did you get bit by a wild animal?" He asked.

The gig was up. "Yes, I did, Sergeant."

"You're going to the hospital for treatment and this knucklehead medic is going to take you," the sergeant replied. "Don't you know it's against regulation to interfere with wild animals?"

"No, Sergeant, I did not," I replied. I had always been celebrated for doing those things, and it never occurred to me that I could get in serious trouble.

Before I left for the hospital, everyone started sharing stories about how horrible the rabies vaccine was.

"They give you shots in the stomach," someone told me.

I started to get nervous. I had a healthy respect for needles, and shots in the stomach did not appeal to me. Since the medic was new, he got lost on the way to the hospital, which gave me plenty of time to think about my current predicament. By the time we arrived at emergency room, I had worked myself up. I checked in at the front desk and sat down to wait my turn. I could not take the fear of the unknown anymore, so I went to the desk and asked the nurse about the rabies vaccine. My expression and question must have humored her because she busted out laughing. I don't think she was trying to be mean. She just found humor in my question. She apologized for laughing and told me now to worry.

I still did.

Eventually, I got my shots. They no longer gave shots in the stomach, so I received mine in the rear-end and arm. The two in the rear-end were not pleasant, but I was thankful it was not the alternative. When I got back to the unit, I was threatened with Uniform Code of Military Justice (UCMJ) Article 15, which was nonjudicial punishment but still pretty serious. An Article 15 could affect my pay and a reduction in rank—neither of which I could afford. In the end, they didn't give me an Article 15, but I did get a severe lecture from the commander. I think I escaped an Article 15 because I was a temporarily assigned National Guard as opposed to permanent party active duty. When I got back to Charleston, I still had to get several more shots. I decided my days of messing around with wildlife were over. I also met my first son, Marc, which was an amazing day. Even if I was scared to be a father, I was determined to be a good one.

A short time after Marc was born, I had to go on permanent active duty. Germany was my first assignment. I also turned in my first new vehicle to the credit company because we could not afford the payments. On top of everything else, my credit was ruined. Even so, the move to active duty was a turning point in my life.

Lesson Sixteen

Just because you stray from God's purpose and make poor decisions, that does not mean God abandons you in your foolishness. God gave you free will, and you'll sometimes make bad decisions. God still loves you and can work in your new situation if you let him.

"For all have sinned and fall short of the Glory of God" (Rom. 3:23).

This verse is applicable here, too, "And we know that God causes everything to work together for the good of those who love God, and are called according to his purpose for them" (Rom. 8:28).

Chapter 10

Prayers Work

"When I pray, coincidences happen, and when I don't,
they don't."
—William Temple

My mother has always been a prayer warrior. Not only has she always prayed for us, but she also has always involved her church family by requesting prayer for those she loves and things that are important to her. She prayed over my siblings and me for years—and continues to—and those prayers have blessed us.

I arrived in Germany in the fall of 1988. I was sent to Nurnberg, the 1st Armored Division's Headquarters. There, I found out I was assigned to Warner Barracks, home of the 1st Armored Division's Bulldog Brigade, in Bamberg, Germany. That was an armored tank brigade with mechanized infantry battalions. I was assigned to 1/54 Infantry battalion. LTC "Iron" Mike McGee was our battalion commander.

My small family stayed in Charleston while I was stationed in Germany. We needed to figure the new phase of our life as a family.

I was reduced to private because the Army did not recognize the SP4 rank I attained in the Guard. So, money was scarce. Since I lived in the barracks, I sent most of my paycheck home to my family.

I drifted away from God prior to Germany, but I drifted back to Him again due to necessity. I had a difficult time at first, but I adjusted okay. We had a good set of platoon leadership. My Platoon Sergeant was a good man, he had a great family and he invited us over to his house every now and then, so we could get out of the barracks.

I had a mixture of good and bad roommates. One roommate did not like me at all. I think he saw me as a weak, religious type. The Army didn't care for my roommate. He got forced out—or chaptered—from the Army because of less-than-honorable circumstances. Because he was in the process of being chaptered out, leadership did not want to deal with him. So, I had to bear with him.

In Germany, I learned being an infantry soldier was not the awesome warrior job I imagined. We were in peacetime. So, we guarded things a lot and did not get to do much shooting or other cool infantry stuff. During peacetime, an infantry unit has an abundance of soldiers with nothing to do, so we did other tasks, including painting rocks. There were times, however, when we went to the field.

The Grafenwoehr Training area was one of my first deployments while I was in Germany. I was an infantryman riding in the back of a M113 APC. We performed a live fire exercise. At one point, we had to dismount and make it to the live fire area on foot. Then, we all had to lie in the prone position and shoot at pop-up targets. The APCs behind us shot .50 caliber machine guns at the same targets. The targets were about 300 meters away, and our goal was to shoot each target as it came up. If we missed a target, it fell on its own and another target popped up closer to us. The better our aim was, the farther we could keep the targets away from us. If we had a poor collective shooting, the targets progressively got closer to our unit.

We did fine keeping the targets at bay until we heard a loud chainsaw-type noise in the sky. A radio-controlled drone, typically used as a target for the Vulcan Air Defense weapon system, flew toward us from down range. The drones were large and made of Styrofoam. They were meant to be shot at by a much larger M163 Vulcan Air Defense rotary 20mm cannon, which shoots at a rate of three thousand rounds per minute. As the drone came toward us, we could not resist shooting at it. We adjusted our fire up to include the track mounted .50 calibers. Since the drone was a moving target, it was difficult to hit with small arms. Even when we did hit it, we could not knock it out of the sky because the bullets only put small holes in the wings. We had to hit the engine or the guy flying it by remote control in order to bring the drone down. To our disappointment, none of us were able to shoot it down; it flew over our heads and passed us.

When we looked back at the ground targets, they had advanced so much that they were in front of us. We forgot about them because of the drone. We all shot at the targets as fast as we could. The .50 caliber, track-mounted, machine gun to my left side also helped. When the machine gunner saw the targets were right in front of us, he adjusted his fire too low and he stitched the ground between another solder and me. All I could do was put my head down. I saw tracer fire and felt dirt flying all around me. I don't know how I didn't get hit. If I had, I would have been killed or severely maimed.

After the machine gunner stopped firing, I got up and started shouting. My platoon sergeant came over to calm me down. Eventually, I calmed down, but that was my first close call at being killed.

Lesson Seventeen

Prayers are powerful; pray hard for the ones you love. When my mother dies, I may not be far behind because I think her prayers for me have kept me alive on many occasions. Don't underestimate

41

the power of your prayers. Thank you, Mom and Christina, for your constant prayers.

"Do not be anxious about anything, but in everything by prayer and supplication with thanksgiving let your requests be made known to God" (Phil. 4:6).

Chapter 11

Another Close Call and Answered Prayers

"Prayer delights God's ear; it melts His heart; and opens His hand. God cannot deny a praying soul."
—Thomas Watson

After about a year in Germany by myself, my family finally made it to Germany, and we moved off post. We found an apartment in the small town of Struellendorf, which is a few kilometers outside of Bamberg. Our apartment was on top of a German stamp collector's shop. The owner was very good to us, and we became friends. The owner and his wife had a son and a daughter. We often did things together. The man was very kind and even loaned us money to buy a used car I needed in order to get to and from work. The German people have really big hearts.

That was a good time for us. While we were extremely tight on money at first, things got better when I was promoted to Private First Class, and then Specialist 4. But money was still tight, nonetheless. Marc was a toddler. And my wife became pregnant again. Brian, my second son, was born in Bamberg, Germany. Our family grew, but I am not sure my wife and I ever loved each other; we just did what we had to do.

I was doing well in my unit, and on another maneuver in Grafenwoehr, I was promoted to .50 caliber machine gunner. It was winter at the time, and the cold temperatures were brutal. It

43

was so cold one day that my machine gun only fired a single shot the first time I fired it. I checked that it was in automatic mode, and it was. Then, I checked the headspace and timing. On a .50 caliber, the barrel must be screwed in just the right amount—the headspace—and also set the timing at the rear of the weapon for the gun to fire correctly. The headspace and timing and both were okay. So, I tried to fire again. Four attempts later, and the weapon only shot one bullet at a time. By the fifth try, after a short delay, the gun fired again. It slowly picked up speed until it fired like it should. It was so cold that the break free—lubricant or oil—we used on the bolt of the weapon froze. That hindered the weapon from firing until the break free heated up enough to allow the gun to shoot fully automatic.

Once I got the weapon firing, we gathered as a platoon and moved down range on a live fire. As we moved, each M113 scanned its lane for large targets that resembled vehicles. My vehicle moved a little too far forward as we engaged targets. I realized that when I looked back to the right to see where the other M113 was, and I could not find him until the target between us went down. The M113's gun was pointed at my vehicle when the target fell. I stared down the barrel of his machine gun. He had been seconds from firing. That was another very close call. Had he engaged the target, the shooter would have also hit my vehicle, and I had half my body sticking out of the top.

Lesson

Refer to previous lesson. Prayers work.

Chapter 12

More Answered Prayers

"Fervent prayers produce phenomenal results."
—Woodrow Kroll

We went to Hoenfels on another deployment. I was in the back of an armored personnel carrier, and we were there to qualify as an infantry company. We were not on a live fire range like Grafenwoehr, but it was a large training area for wargames that required blanks in our weapons. The vehicle came to a halt, and the back opened. My squad leader stuck his head in and yelled at my friend Jack and me. "You guys get your asses out here." So, we did. We were stopped in an enemy's potential choke point area. In the scenario, the enemy could try to get into the valley being defended by our unit. The choke point had several rows of razor sharp concertina wire across it. The idea was to slow the enemy, so they could be engaged. We were assigned to man an observation post (OP) that overlooked the choke point. We had to watch and report back to our commander.

We were given some MREs and a radio. Nothing happened yet, so my buddy and I sat and talked while it started to get dark. He threw MRE wrappers that still had food in them on the ground. I told him that was not a great idea because of the boars. He didn't agree and continued to throw food on the ground.

I suggested we take turns sleeping, so someone always watched the choke point. I volunteered to take the first watch. It was bitterly cold and miserable. About an hour later, I woke my buddy up and told him it was his turn. So, he got up, and I went to sleep.

I heard the radio at some point, and my friend didn't answer. I realized he was asleep. I shook my friend awake. He was our squad's automatic weapon (SAW) gunner, and he had a SAW with a full belt of 5.56 blank ammunition in it. When I shook him, he bolted up right and grabbed his SAW. He shot the entire belt of ammunition. In the flashes of light that came from the muzzle, we saw boars all around us. They were eating his discarded food. The boars were not cute. They were big and hairy, and had large, sharp tusks that stuck out of their mouths. The boars didn't seem bothered by the gunshots but did eventually leave. I am not sure how we were not attacked.

Lesson

Refer to previous lesson. Prayers work.

Chapter 13

Divine Appointments

"The superior man is quiet and calm, waiting for the appointments of heaven, while the mean man walks in dangerous paths, looking for lucky occurrences."
—Confucius

It was often miserable out in the field. Rain, snow, and cold weather had me rethinking my choice to join the infantry. I remember being in the field and rain and sleet coming down sideways due to high winds. I began to think about another line of work. When I heard the command sergeant major (CSM) was looking for a graphic illustrator to move to the S-3, or Operations shop, I thought it might be a good option to improve my quality of life in the infantry. At the time, I did a lot of artwork off duty. It was nothing serious. I did cartoon character paintings in acrylic paint. I was no Michelangelo, but my paintings were not bad. Artistic abilities ran in my family.

One day, I was scheduled for guard duty in the motor pool. I thought the CSM would be by at some point to check the guard post. So, I brought some of my paintings with me. While I was at my guard post, I saw the CSM heading my direction. I laid out my paintings. When he got there, he asked me about the paintings. After a short conversation, he asked if I was interested in the illustrator job. He arranged for me to be on the Battalion S-3 (senior

47

operations officer) M113 crew and to do artwork when I was not deployed. That was a good trade-off for me. So, I started doing artwork that consisted of drawing and painting the battalion and division crests on signs and vehicles.

Our battalion, 1/54 Infantry, was scheduled to deactivate, but the situation in Iraq was worsening. Saddam Hussein attacked and occupied Kuwait. I am not sure if that was related to events in Iraq, but our infantry battalion was re-designated to 6–6 Infantry and directed to turn in our M113s. We transitioned to Bradley Fighting Vehicles (BFVs). The BFVs were a significant improvement over the M113s. The M113 only had a .50 caliber machine gun, but the BFV had a 25mm cannon that shot both high explosive rounds and sabot rounds with a push of a button. The sabot round could pierce steel and other hard objects. A high-density metal dart, for lack of a better way of describing it, about the size of a Bic pen, was incased in plastic and made up the projectile. When the projectile left the barrel, the plastic fell away and the metal dart flew on a much flatter trajectory than the high explosive round. It used kinetic energy to pierce hulls of enemy vehicles. Having both high explosive rounds and sabot rounds in the same cannon was a great capability.

On top of that, we also had a coaxially mounted 7.62mm machine gun and a tube launched optically-tracked wire-guided (TOW) missile launcher. The TOW launcher had two missiles that were capable of killing any known armor on the battlefield at a max range of 3,750 meters. Plus, it could still carry troops like the M113. The troops had portholes to fire personal weapons through. The BFVs also provided really good optics, including thermal optics, which were better than the M1 Abrams main battle tank in the brigade.

Our newly re-designated battalion went to Vilseck, Germany, to train on the new weapons system. To qualify, we had to learn each position in the BFV. We had to qualify as driver, gunner, vehicle commander, and dismount. As newly trained infantrymen, we had to be proficient in each position. The training lasted several weeks. When we weren't training, we had to pull duty in the deployed headquarters. I was assigned night duty one night, and it turned out to be a divine moment in my life.

I pulled duty in the deployed headquarters one night. After the normal evening activities, I was left alone to monitor the phones and radios. One of our unit computers had a game called Gunship. It was a helicopter videogame. I was playing when LTC McGee came in to check on things. He saw what I was doing, and he struck up a conversation that significantly changed my life. We talked about the game and flying helicopters, and he suggested I look into Warrant Officer Candidate School and flight training. He said I didn't need a college degree for the position and that many enlisted soldiers could transition to be a helicopter pilot.

I loved that he gave me his time, but I also thought he was crazy. That conversation, however, was a divine appointment orchestrated by God. After LTC McGee left, the idea stuck with me. Every time I decided the idea was crazy, I eventually came back to it. I believe God's divine intervention kept the idea in my head, so I eventually started my journey to become an Army helicopter pilot in spite of all the odds against it.

Lesson Eighteen

Divine appointments are real; don't miss them. God puts people in our paths who we need, or sometimes they need us.

"There is an appointed time for everything. And there is a time for every event under heaven—A time to give birth and a time to die; A time to plant and a time to uproot what is planted" (Eccles. 3:1–2).

Chapter 14

Be Obedient

"Don't bother to give God instructions, just report for duty."
—Corrie ten Boom

One of the first steps to become a pilot was to see if my Armed Forces Vocational Aptitude Battery (ASVAB) score was high enough. One of the components of the ASVAB is the GT section, which I think loosely relates to an IQ score. You needed a 110 GT to be an officer. I thought my journey was already over, or at least delayed, while I worked to get my score high enough. When I went to the education center to check, my GT was exactly 110. God was in it.

I also had to take the Army Flight Aptitude Selection Test (AFAST). I needed a score of 90 or higher to pass. There were two hundred questions on the test, in seven separate sections. If I failed the test, I had to wait six months before I could take it again. If I failed the retake, I could never take the test again. I was not the best test taker, but I was committed to giving it my best shot.

Warner Barracks was a small base, but it did have a small airfield with a couple of UH-1H Huey helicopters. I arranged to go out and talk to the pilots, which was a smart move. Chief Asbell was the senior pilot and was kind enough to speak with me. Beforehand, I purchased a book on the AH-64 Apache Attack helicopter. It had more pictures than words. That's how foolish and immature I was, but Chief Asbell was kind enough to give me ideas on other, more appropriate study material. He suggested Field Manual (FM) 1–203 *Fundamentals of Flight*, FM 1–240 *Instrument Flight for Army Aviators*, and the *AFAST* study guide. Those books were exactly what I needed, but I didn't have great study skills.

I spent three months studying for the AFAST test. That was the first time I ever took academics seriously. Every moment that I had available, I spent preparing for that test.

The day of the test quickly approached, and I walked into the testing center feeling unprepared. After I finished the test, I waited for the bad news. I was sure I did not pass the flight aptitude test. To my absolute surprise, I scored 139, which was significantly higher than the minimum and very close to the maximum score. All my hard work paid off.

Then, I had to take a flight physical, which I passed. I also had to get letters of recommendation from my Battalion Commander and supervisor. At the time, Major Curtis was the officer in charge of the S3 section. He asked me to draft letter, and he would edit it. I didn't even spell Charleston, South Carolina, correctly, and he noticed. He was kind enough to edit and sign the document. I then had my flight packet together.

I went to Spain for military maneuvers with my unit. The Warrant Officer selection board decided my fate while I was gone. As soon as I got back, I ran to the education center to make the call back to the United States and find out. The person on the other end of the phone said I was selected to attend Warrant Officer Candidate School and Flight School. I could not believe it. Did they know I was a high school drop out?!

I was scheduled to attend Warrant Officer Candidate School (WOCS) in about six months. We got the news, however, that 7th Corps, our 1st Armored Division, 3rd Bulldog Brigade, and 6–6 infantry were deploying to the Kingdom of Saudi Arabia (KSA). Flight school had to wait. We prepared for war.

Our preparations were hard. We did physical training (PT) in Mission Oriented Protective Posture (MOPP) gear, which was a protective suit and gas mask that protected us from chemical agents Saddam Hussein might use. We prepped our BFVs and loaded them on trains for the long ride to the shipping ports. Then, we were off to Dhahran, KSA. We flew there on a commercial airline.

We decided that my wife, Marc, and Brian should go home to Charleston. There was no telling how long I would be deployed. I was hopeful that when I returned, I would be going to flight school in Alabama. So, my family left shortly after I deployed to KSA. As a family, we continued to do okay but not great. My wife and I continued to exist. The boys were growing though, getting bigger with each day.

Lesson Nineteen

Be obedient when God gives you direction and opportunity. We have free will and can elect not to follow God's prompting, but we will miss a lot of the goodness He has for us if we do.

I had plenty of reasons to avoid all the work that went into my flight packet. The odds of getting in were stacked against me. The reality, however, was I should not have been picked.

"Walk in obedience to all that the Lord your God has commanded you, so that you may live and prosper and prolong your days in the land that you will possess" (Deut. 5:33).

Lesson Twenty

Lean not on your own understanding, but trust in God's plan. Do not make assumptions about what God can or will do. Our God is not bound by space and time. He knows what you will need before you ask Him.

"Trust in the LORD with all your heart and lean not on your own understanding" (Prov. 3:5).

This section of the book may be a little tough to read because it details my first experience in combat. I experienced some difficult times because of it. I included it because it's part of my story. God protected me and guided me in profound ways. So, forgive anything graphic.

Chapter 15
Rational Fear: God Is Still Sovereign

"The remarkable thing about God is that when you fear God, you fear nothing else, whereas if you do not fear God, you fear everything else."
—Oswald Chambers

My unit arrived in KSA, and we got stuck in a tent city outside of Dhahran. We had to wait for our equipment to arrive before we could deploy to the Iraq border. We kept ourselves busy with whatever we could.

I experienced quite a culture shock, too. I had never been to the Middle East, and it was different from anything I knew. Christmas came, and we were still in the tent city waiting on our equipment.

After a couple of months in country, our BFVs arrived. We left for the Port of Dhahran to get our equipment. That was the first time we got off our compound. We saw the towns and people of KSA. Everything was different: the way people dressed and their customs.

We loaded our BFVs and M1 tanks on flatbed trucks, or lowboys, that took us to Wadi Al Batin, our staging area.

Our crew finished loading the BFV. It was already on the flatbed, but we had to secure it with load binders. We attached one end of the load binder to the hard point on the BFV and the other to the flatbed. There was a lot of tension in the load binder, and it had to be locked in place. We used a steel sissy bar that was four to six feet long and put it on the load binder arm as leverage. Then, four men pulled on the bar, and I pushed to secure it in place. When it locked into place, before one of the other guys removed the sissy bar, I turned to jump off the lowboy. As I jumped, I heard the load binder give away and the sissy bar shot in my direction. As I was in midair, I felt the bar go by my head; it skimmed the side of my head. I rolled when I hit the ground, and everyone thought the bar had hit me. If the bar had come any closer to me, I am not sure I would have survived.

We got out to Wadi Al Batin and set up a forward operating base (FOB). That's when it got difficult. We waited for weeks, not knowing if we were going to fight the Iraqis or if we were going to sit for months to keep the Iraqis from coming into KSA. When we were not sleeping, we typically had to do some sort of duty to keep us busy and out of trouble. The worst thing I had to do was burn feces and urine. The latrines used fifty-gallon drums that were cut in half and put under the sitting positions in the latrine. I had to use fifty percent gasoline and fifty percent diesel to burn the poop. If I put too much gasoline in, the fuel would burn faster than the material. If I put too much diesel in, it would burn too slow. Once I got it burning, I then had to stir the mixture the entire time. It was not a pleasant duty, and the smell was horrible. When I finished, my uniform reeked. The Battalion S3 changed out, and we got a new officer in charge (OIC), but he didn't last long. He had an accidental discharge from his weapon. He was removed and Major H., took over. He was a tanker.

The air war eventually started, and we had our chance to go across the border. We listened to aircraft fly overhead for strike missions for weeks. Then, it was our turn to fight the enemy. At first, our enemy contact was minimal. We came across small groups of enemy soldiers and exchanged fire. Our firepower was far superior to theirs, so the fight was more or less one-sided. The next morning, we were in temporary battle positions, and we could see an Iraqi solider moving toward us. There was a lot of chatter over the radio; we tried to figure out what he was doing. So, one of the other BFVs fired warning shots, and the guy got down. Then he got back up, and the same gunner killed him.

The man took three shots to the head/eye. His brains were everywhere. That was the first time I saw someone be killed in battle. It was not pleasant. We searched his body and found pictures of his family. That incident still bothers me to this day. He didn't even have shoes on his feet.

Later that day, we had a larger group give up to us and we had a problem keeping up with the prisoners of war (POWs) we collected. We passed them off to units to our rear and continued the mission.

Our first big fight was in Al Bussayyah, a city and large enemy logistical site guarded by a mechanized infantry battalion, tank company, and some others. By that time, all our battalions had turned into task forces with both Bradley and Abrams tank companies. We did that mission with three Bradley companies and two Abrams companies. The fight started in the early morning hours, and the weather was bad with low cloud ceilings. As our battalion moved forward, the Iraqis shot at us, and we returned fire. They shot larger guns and tanks, and it was the first time I really wondered if I would get hit by enemy fire. We watched them shoot and wondered what they were aiming at. Even so, we took them out as fast as we saw them. Our weapons' ranges were significantly better, so in most cases, their fire was ineffective.

While we were still out a bit, we maneuvered our BFV over a small ridge that stood between us and the city. As we climbed the ridge and came over the top, we saw a T-55 tank with its gun trained on us. We were oblique to him with our main gun pointed in another direction. He had the drop on us, and even though we tried to get our gun around, we all braced for impact. We thought we were dead. All of a sudden, the T-55 exploded. An Abrams tank crew saw him in time and killed him before he could get a round off at us. That was another close call, and I experienced God's unearned protection.

We continued the battle and did a pretty good job of engaging everything on the outskirts of the city. We went around the town to the far side. I saw a lot of white flags go up. Then we got the call that 6–6 infantry was to clear the inside of the town. We had to go back and fight through the town. We repositioned and started our attack. My Bradley went down one street, and I saw a combat engineer vehicle (CEV) coming down the street beside us. It was a block away. A CEV is an engineer vehicle on an M60 tank chassis, with a 165mm demolition gun on top. The gun is powerful and used to knock out defensive positions. They were knocking down buildings with it. One building was between us when the gunner took his shot. A good bit of that building ended up on our BFV.

We continued to fight through the town, engaging anyone who resisted and taking others as prisoners. As we finished the fight, a helicopter flew overhead and spotted a bunker complex nearby. My BFV was one of a few free to respond. We raced over to find a bunch of Iraqis surrendering. There were so many that we had to dismount to help. At one point, I ended up applying first aid on one guy who had shrapnel wounds. I gave him one of my rations. The Iraqis were shocked to receive such treatment. We medically treated them and gave them food, which they desperately needed.

After we handed over the POWs to the Military Police, we came back together and continued the mission. We made our way further north, toward the Republican Guards Medina Division. Along the way, we saw a lot of dogs. They had been with the Iraqis, and scattered during the air campaign. Some of my worst war memories included the dogs eating dead people. It was nothing to see a dog with a severed hand or other body part in its mouth. The dogs became a problem because they grew accustomed to eating people and were packing up. When we stopped to rest, we had to send out killer teams to get rid of the dogs. It was sad for me because it became more sport than necessity for some people.

Our vehicle commander and battalion S3 pulled out his side arm and shot dogs when he saw them. One time, a mother dog and her pups were running around, and he pulled out his .45 caliber weapon to shoot them. He hit one pup in the stomach and its guts hung out. I lost a lot of respect for him because he seemed to have fun with it. It was more sport than necessity, and he was a poor shot.

We continued until we got to the Medina Division. The fight was on. The Medina Division was one of the famed and elite units in the Iraqi Army, but they did not last long against our firepower. An Abrams super sabot round could make a catastrophic kill at 4,000 meters, and the Bradley TOW missile could hit any vehicle they had at a max range of 3,750 meters. The T-72 was the best tank the Republican Guard had; it had a max effective range of 2,000 meters. It was not a fair fight at all, but that's how we wanted it. We didn't have to blow up many of their tanks before the Republican Guard gave up. We beat the best Saddam Hussein had.

At some point, we crossed into Kuwait. We continued into Kuwait and turned north towards Basrah, Iraq. We passed through all the oil fires the Iraqis set in their retreat.

By then, we had been fighting and moving for a few days. We passed through northern Kuwait back into Iraq and continued the fight toward Basrah. The cease fire was called, so we stopped and formed a defensive line to await orders. We were told to avoid engaging with the enemy. As the night went on, we saw a new enemy unit assuming fighting positions and positioning vehicles about 2,000 meters in front of us. The unit was mechanized, and a pickup truck seemed to be the command vehicle, going to each one. As we watched the scene unfold, we were concerned they had not gotten the ceasefire message, and there would be unnecessary bloodshed.

By the time morning came, our brigade commander flew in and assisted because he didn't want an incident. We then moved three of our five companies toward the enemy. We left two companies in reserve, just in case things went poorly, so they could be flexed where needed. As we crept forward, I heard the radio traffic. One unit reported movement by the enemy, or another unit reported in their area. No one knew what to make of that. As we moved forward, no one shot from any direction. As we moved inside their weapons ranges, we heard the excitement and anxiety on the radio. Then, as if on cue, the enemies produced white flags and put their hands up. That allowed them to be captured without giving up—at least in their minds. By waiting to be overwhelmed by our larger and more capable force, as opposed to coming to us with a white flag, they saved a little face among themselves.

That created a problem. We had a lot of POWs to process. We approached them and gradually took them in and secured them. There were so many POWs that the two reserve companies had to assist. One of the companies sped across the desert to get there and did not slow down enough to cross a berm. One of the platoon leader's Bradley hit the berm in a way that sent the twenty-seven-ton vehicle airborne for a moment. When it came crashing down on the other side, so did the platoon leader's face. He landed on top of the steel armored surface. His face was pretty crushed. Medics were called in to work on him while the rest of us continued to process the POWs.

Later that day, the platoon leader with the smashed face woke up in the POW cage with the rest of the prisoners. He had a darker complexion, perhaps Italian ancestry, and the Bradley crewmember's uniform was green and similar to the enemies' uniforms. With all the blood and his destroyed face, the medics lost track of him. When the platoon leader woke up, he started yelling. The POW guards finally figured it out and got him out of the POW area.

There were other close calls. My Bradley crew called in mortar fire from our 4.2 inch mortar platoon at targets that were approximately one thousand meters away. We were on top of the Bradley, listening to the rounds go overhead, much like you hear in the movies. One round was especially loud and landed about fifty meters from us. It was phosphorous as opposed to high explosive (HE) and that's what saved us. Had it been an HE round, we would have, at the very least, had shrapnel wounds.

That was it. The war was over, and the waiting began. I spent my time studying aerodynamics as I focused once again on flight school. I studied whenever I had time. We sat and waited and occasionally moved to another area until it was time to go home. We were able to make an occasional morale call back to the States, but that was a painful process. We got in the back of a five-ton truck and rode for hours to big AT&T phone tents that looked like circus tents. Then, we got in line and waited a couple more hours. Once we got to a phone, we had fifteen minutes whether we connected or not. Cell phones were not the norm back then, so if a loved one was not home, we didn't get to talk. And if we did, the call was extremely expensive. Then, we drove the couple hours back to our forward operating base (FOB). So, just making a phone call was an all-day, very expensive event.

We finally made it back to KSA and waited again. We spent most days turning in gear we had drawn there or we just hung out. One of the highlights of waiting to go home was that I was awarded the Combat Infantryman's Badge (CIB), which was rare up to that point in the Army. The small handful of soldiers who had a CIB were old Vietnam veterans, a handful of people from Operation Urgent Furry in Grenada, and Operations Just Cause in Panama. I say it was rare, but it is not so rare anymore. We had fought an infantry/armor war, so it became pretty common to have a CIB. I, however, was still proud of it.

Eventually, it was time for us to go back to Germany. When I arrived in Germany, I moved into the barracks since my family had returned to Charleston. I made the most of my time by studying and exercising for flight school and preparing for the Expert Infantryman's Badge (EIB) testing. The EIB was a coveted badge. Back in those days, it was difficult to pass the EIB test. Only a small percentage of the unit that tested actually passed. There was not a lot of room for error. We were only allotted a couple of retests if we messed up. I worked hard during training. So, I trained hard, and when testing time came, I passed and was awarded the EIB. That was another proud day for me. EIBs were less common than the CIBs.

I eventually got a new flight school class date and returned to the States. I picked up my family in Charleston, and we went to Ft. Rucker, Alabama. That was where the Army's Warrant Officer Candidate School (WOCS) and flight school were located. It was not long before we discovered that Kevin, my third child, was on the way. My family kept growing, and we were finally moving in a positive direction.

Lesson Twenty-One

Rational fear is good because it forces us to react in ways that preserve life, but it is also real that you could lose your life. God is sovereign when it comes to rational fear and life-threatening situations. I believe I was protected because my purpose had not yet been fulfilled. God still had work for me to do, and He knew I would be obedient in His calling. I also had prayer warriors, including my mom, praying for me.

"So do not fear, for I am with you; do not be dismayed, for I am your God. I will strengthen you and help you; I will uphold you with my righteous right hand" (Isa. 41:10).

Chapter 16

The Story of the Rose

*"I love to think of nature as an unlimited broadcasting sta-
tion, through which God speaks to us every hour, if we will
only tune in."*
—*George Washington Carver*

God speaks in many ways and forms, and if you listen, you will
hear him. While I was in Iraq, my mother was worried sick
about what might happen to me, as you can imagine. This is what
she said about God speaking to her:

It all started with Hurricane Hugo, the storm hit Charleston,
South Carolina, in September 1989.

I grew up in Miami, and it seemed like we had a hurricane every
year, but we never had a ton of damage. Plus, I was a child, so I
didn't have any responsibilities. The hurricanes never scared me.

Hurricane Hugo was a different situation all together. I was not
prepared. After the storm left Charleston, I didn't recognize anything. We walked over to a friend's house. I noticed that even with
all the destruction, she had a red rose in the yard. I looked around
for petals on the ground and anything else that might be wrong with
the plant, but I saw nothing.

Immediately, God spoke to me and told me it was a significant
moment for me, I just didn't understand what it meant. I knew God

wanted to tell me something. I even went home to call my mother and tell her. It left a lasting impression on her as well.

A few years later, we experienced a different type of storm— Desert Storm. My son deployed to Saudi Arabia before the war started, and we had very little communication. The military set up phones, so soldiers could call home sometimes, but there were always long lines for the phones, so my son couldn't call home often.

I was working the day the ground war started. Craig's wife was the one who informed me. I told myself I wouldn't cry until I left work. When I got in my car, I went straight to church. I cried the entire way. I got to church for the Wednesday night prayer meeting. While I was in the church, there, with my eyes closed, was a perfect red rose. I opened my eyes and closed them again, but I still saw the rose.

God said, "Not a petal was hurt in the storm." God was referring to Desert Storm and my son. My mind flashed back to that red rose after Hurricane Hugo.

I immediately felt peace. I went home and told my mother that God left the image of the rose on my heart, and she was also at peace.

Lesson Twenty-Two

God speaks to us in many different ways, but we have to listen for Him. We have to seek Him in our daily lives. If we do, He will show up in big and meaningful ways. Sometimes we have to wait to understand something God puts on our hearts. When you receive a message from God, write it down or use some other way to remember it. God may use it when we least expect it. Sometimes we have to stop and smell the roses.

"My sheep hear my voice, and I know them, and they follow me. I give them eternal life, and they will never perish, and no one will snatch them out of my hand" (John 10:27–28).

Me as a baby.

Gammy and Grandad.

My Mom and me.

Me at about 4 years old.

Nadara, Me, Craig and Jaime (bottom).

The deer I caught in 1987.

Getting promoted to Private again in Germany.

My infantry platoon in front of a M113 Armored Personnel Carrier 1988.

Me in the back of my Bradley in Iraq studying Aerodynamics.

Waiting for the war to start.

AH-1F Cobra pilot in Korea.

Standing by for a mission.

On the deck of the USS Eisenhower headed to Haiti for Operation Restore/Uphold Democracy.

Making friends with the locals in Haiti.

Gammy, Grandad and I on his 84 birthday, about a year before he died.

Christina, Alana and Aaron.

Jaime, Nadara, Me, Christina, and Craig on our Wedding day.

Gary Sinise visiting my Unit on Hunter Army Airfield while I was a commander there.

My new aircraft, the MH-60 DAP (Direct Action Penetrator) with the 3/160th SOAR.

Me in front of the DAP during aircraft qualification training in 2004.

All five of my boys!

My son Brian and I at his Air Force Basic Training Graduation.

Christina and I in uniform.

Kevin, me and Ryan, my dive buddies at the Eagles Nest!

Me and my bestie!

Passing through Marrakesh during my work travels.

Making Thanksgiving dinner with my best friend Joe.

My family doing one of my favorite things!

Bradley Thomas McAteer.

Tucker and I during his scuba certification in 2019.

Chapter 17

God Equips You for His Calling

"God doesn't call the equipped, son. God equips the called. And you have been called."
—Rick Yancy

My family and I made it to Ft Rucker, Alabama, home of Army aviation. We were fortunate to get housing on base, which made life easier. Our little family was doing well, and Kevin was on his way.

While I waited for the next class to start, I was in snowbird status, which gave me time to catch up with my family after I had been overseas for eight months.

Warrant Officer Candidate School eventually started, and boy, that was an eye opening experience. The school was shorter than basic training but more intense. My typical day included a very early wake-up time, strenuous PT, and then academics, which was followed by more PT.

The barracks were a mess every day I got back. Oftentimes, a warrant officer candidates (WOCs) salad was on the floor. A WOC salad is when everyone's stuff was dumped into one big pile on the floor. We had to sift through everything to retrieve our things. Then we had to organize it all again for inspection. That took more of our time and stressed attention to detail. While difficult, I didn't

73

particularly mind WOC school. It was my path to become a heli-copter pilot.

We did have a lot of fun, though too; pranks were practically encouraged. We were always punished for the pranks, but we'd be punished for some sort of infraction anyway. We built a closet in the office doorway of the Training, Advising Counseling (TAC) Officer's Offices, making it look like a broom closet when they opened their office door. We got plywood for the walls which we painted the same color of the office walls. Then, we filled the space with booms, mops, and other cleaning supplies.

Another time, we filled the office, floor to ceiling, with balloons. We also stacked cardboard boxes from floor to ceiling to fill their office. One time, we even put plastic on the floor and turned one office into a beach. Make no mistake, though, WOC school was not all fun and games. Each candidate had to carry a large wallet that had a pink slip and a green slip in it. At any point, someone could pull your slip, and there would be hell to pay.

After a couple of weeks in school, I got a message that my mother had been diagnosed with breast cancer. As I contemplated what to do, she told me to stay in school and that she had enough support at home to make it through her treatments. She also said her prognosis was good. So, I stayed in school. My classmates were very gracious and pooled their money together for a card and flowers. As I continued in school, Mom did well and pulled through her cancer.

When I went to WOC school and flight school, things were a little different than they are now. I attended WOC School at Ft. Rucker on Ghost Rider Street. It was in the old World War II bar-racks. After graduation, we had to wear the WOC rank for the entire flight school, but now WOCS get promoted to Warrant Officer One before flight training begins. On top of that, even after graduation, we were on lockdown for another six weeks while in flight school.

Graduation from WOC school did not change much, except that we attended flight academics and actually got to fly.

Since we were still treated as WOCs and were learning to become pilots, it was still pretty rough. The TACs continued to focus on our time management and attention to detail. They knew those skills were also important to being a pilot.

To save time, I preset my combination lock so I could easily open it. That allowed me to turn it to its final number and unlock it. Unfortunately, the TACs knew my trick. One day, I came back to the barracks and walked down the hall to my room. I noticed someone's flight helmet was sitting on top of their boots in the center of the hallway. Their panel markers (orange signal markers) were also hanging from the ceiling. "That sucks for someone," I thought. When I entered my room, I realized it was my stuff. My locker was open, and all of its contents were scattered across the floor.

Once I finally made it out of lock-down, I continued on to flight school and lived at home with my family. The boys were growing more and more every day. My wife and I were doing okay. I started flying in an old UH-1 Huey, which was fascinating for me.

Craig and I had a teenage fascination with the Vietnam War. The Huey was a symbol of that war. It was amazing to fly the Huey from the start, but it was quite the challenge learning to hover.

When hovering a helicopter, you try to stay stationary over a spot on the ground. In order to do that, control inputs need to be very small—to the point you almost *think* the direction you want to go instead of inputting an actual control movement. That is especially true for the cyclic. The cyclic is the stick between the pilot's legs. It is used to control a helicopter's direction. When you push the stick forward, the helicopter goes forward. When you move the stick it to the right, the helicopter flies to the right. The collective is the stick to the left side of the pilot. It is for power. When you pull the stick up, the helicopter gains power. While hovering, that power input allows the aircraft to climb in altitude. The pedals are used to counteract the torque that is caused by the main rotor. If the rotor turns to the left, the fuselage, or body, of the aircraft wants to move in the opposite direction. The tail rotor helps to push against that opposition force. The pedals control the tail rotor.

When hovering, all control inputs need to be very small. Otherwise, the helicopter will fly or at least move erratically: up and down, side to side, forward and backward, and the nose will swing back and forth. Controlling the helicopter is challenging at first; but at some point, you get the hang of it, and hovering is no longer a struggle.

Learning to fly directionally is also a challenge because you manipulate equilibrium and adjust to a new one the entire time you are flying. In order to do that, you have to constantly adjust all of the controls. For example, if I wanted to speed up from 100 knots to 120 knots, I would push the cyclic forward. I would also need to increase the power with the collective, or I would begin to descend. Since I added power, I would also need to push in the left pedal to counteract the added torque from pulling in power.

Learning to be a pilot is much more than flying the helicopter, though. In fact, I would say the flying part is not the most difficult part of being a pilot. The most challenging part is knowing aircraft systems, airspace, flying rules, and situational awareness. Those skills make for a good pilot.

Once I made it through basic flying, instruments were my next step. The instrument course taught me how to fly using instruments alone. The reason for that is so we can fly into inclement weather or clouds, when we cannot see outside the aircraft. Instrument flying was a challenge for me because I could no longer trust what my body was telling me. When we fly using visuals, our bodies (proprioceptive) and inner ears (vestibular) give us information that generally agrees with what we see. It's where the phrase, "flying by the seat of your pants," comes from. When you take away visual cues, however, and can only look at instruments, such as the artificial horizon, vertical speed indicator, air speed, and pointers, your inner ear and body can mislead you. It's a lot easier to trust what you see outside the aircraft than several small instruments in the aircraft.

For example, if you enter a sustained aircraft turn, your vestibular system, which is located within your inner ears, will tell your brain that you're turning. This is caused by fluid and hairs in the semicircular canal moving and transmitting this movement to your brain. If you stay in that turn long enough, the fluid and hairs stop sensing movement, and your body thinks you've stopped turning. If you then level the aircraft, you may perceive a turn in the opposite direction because the fluid, which had reached equilibrium, now starts moving again in the opposite direction. That is because the fluid and hairs in your inner ear sense another turn but cannot match it up visually. A pilot may turn in the opposite direction in an attempt to keep the aircraft level. That move is called a graveyard spin for good reason. It has killed a lot of pilots.

We all put in our preferred aircraft preferences for after flight school. The choices included:

- Huey—there were a limited number of UH-1s in the active Army
- Cobra—an attack helicopter, AH-1s were slowly phased out for a newer AH-64
- Apache—an attack helicopter, the AH-64 replaced the AH-1
- Blackhawk—UH-60s were assault helicopters
- Kiowa—OH-58s were scout helicopters

With my infantry background, I wanted to fly attack helicopters, which put the Cobra and Apache at the top of my list. Since I previously flew the Huey and loved every minute of it, I decided on the Cobra because it was one of the legacy aircraft from Vietnam I had read so much about. I also knew that its days were numbered.

I didn't want to miss the opportunity to fly one. Plus, when the aircraft was retired, I would qualify into a new aircraft. When the aircraft assignment list came out, I got the Cobra.

Of all the aircraft I have flown, the Cobra is one of my favorites. It was difficult to fly at first; it hovered at a 40-knot attitude. So, when it came up to a hover, the nose hung low, and I felt like I was about to take off. New pilots naturally want to pull back on the cyclic to level the aircraft. It's supposed to hover with its nose low, however, so pulling back on the cyclic forces the aircraft to go backward. The transmission was also very high, which made the aircraft's center of gravity high.

Switchology made the Cobra difficult to fly as well. There were so many switches and buttons in the aircraft, and it took a long time to figure out which button did what in the aircraft. Not only was the aircraft older than I was, but there were also weapon systems. The Cobra had a 20mm, three-barrel cannon that pointed in the direction the backseat pilot looked. The pilot could look at a target and pull the action switch on the cyclic, then the gun would swivel. The Cobras I flew had two, nineteen, or seven shot rocket pods and TOW missile launchers, which were on the BFV as well.

Night vision goggles were also part of training. I had a near-death experience during that training. Night vision goggle training consists of academics and flying. Flying includes traffic pattern work at one of the stage fields, as well as navigation routes. One of the rules for instructor pilots is that nap of the earth (NOE) routes must be started at a known point and ended at a known point. NOE is when a pilot flies very close to the ground at varying airspeeds. Sometimes the flight takes place between trees and is meant to conceal the aircraft from the enemy. One night, my instructor pilot took me out to fly a NOE route. We were looking for the start point, but we were also running behind. At one point, he thought he saw the NOE route and told me to fly the route. We didn't have time to get to the start point of the route. Doing so turned out to be a mistake.

Flying down the route, we rounded a large grove of trees and then a massive set of power lines were right in front of us. We were both on the controls, trying to stop the aircraft's forward movement. The aircraft was too low, so we could not fly over the power lines. So, we practically had to stand the aircraft on its tail to stop it in time. I am not sure how we managed to avoid the lines, but it rattled the instructor pilot quite a bit. He had me climb up to altitude, and we didn't say a word to each other until I suggested we return to the airfield.

I deployed to Korea for my first operational tour as a helicopter pilot—an AH-1F Cobra pilot. I was also an officer. I never had a back-up plan, but I realized I didn't need one because I had God with me. I still only had a tenth-grade formal education!

Lesson Twenty-Three

God will equip you for His work and your purpose. That does not mean you won't have to work hard. It won't happen overnight, but it can. You have to seek God and be obedient to Him. Don't pass up God's blessings because you don't feel you're equipped to fulfill them. God will equip you for His calling.

"May he equip you with all you need for doing his will. May he produce in you, through the power of Jesus Christ, everything good that is pleasing to him. All glory to him forever and ever! Amen" (Heb. 13:21 NLT).

Chapter 18

Forgiveness (Again) and Grace

"And you know, when you've experienced grace and you feel like you've been forgiven, you're a lot more forgiving of other people. You're a lot more gracious to others."
—Rick Warren

One of the most painful situations in my life relates to divorcing my first wife. Her boyfriend became her second husband. The things they did to my sons and me for the better part of fifteen years has stuck with me. My sinful nature wants me to write about it all, to somehow seek revenge. But I have learned that without God's grace and mercy, I would not be where I am today.

To be fair, there are two sides to every story. I was an immature husband who was selfish at times. From the first Gulf War to flight school and a one-year deployment to Korea, I was gone a lot, and it was hard to maintain a marriage. When I got back from Korea, my wife wanted a divorce. Life got worse.

To be honest, I probably could not write about that part of my past in an objective way. In many ways, I am still working on forgiveness. I chose to forgive, and I am committed to it. In this case, forgiving my ex-wife and her second husband is an ongoing choice because I still see some negative effects it had on my children, who are now adults, and my own painful memories. Forgiveness has freed me from anger and resentment. I still struggle, at times, but for the most part I am free from it. I have moved on to the joy and prosperity God wants for me.

Even now, I occasionally have to set this situation on the altar and forgive again because honestly when I think about it, I feel angry. Sometimes, we have to decide to forgive multiple times. That is the only way to move on and heal. We must deal with what we have done and forgive. We must forgive others and ourselves.

Lesson Twenty-Four

None of us deserve anything good, but I am so thankful I didn't get what I deserved. God's grace is awesome. Since we receive grace so often, we should give it often.

"Let us then with confidence draw near to the throne of grace, that we may receive mercy and find grace to help in time of need" (Heb. 4:16).

Lesson Twenty-Five

We must deal with the garbage in our lives and not always blame things on another person's faults. It's easy to blame someone else for all the bad things in our lives, but it's more useful to examine your own role in the conflict and address it. Sometimes we can achieve that between God and ourselves, but sometimes our actions need to be brought into the light, particularly when other people are involved or have been hurt. Sometimes, we need to confess our sins to our heavenly Father, as well as those we have hurt.

"Therefore, if you are offering your gift at the altar and there remember that your brother or sister has something against you, leave your gift there in front of the altar. First go and be reconciled to them; then come and offer your gift" (Matt. 5:23–24).

Chapter 19

Being Equipped Once Again

"There's nothing more calming in difficult moments than knowing there's someone fighting with you."
—*Mother Teresa*

loved flying the Cobra attack helicopter, but during peace time, there was not a lot of flying. I called my career manager at the Department of the Army and asked to transition to Black Hawks. I did not think I would get it. Once you became an attack pilot, you were committed to the mission. It was very rare for an attack helicopter pilot to become a lift pilot. I asked anyway, and to my surprise I was granted the request on the condition that Ft. Drum, New York, be my next assignment. Fort Drum was considered to be a less-than-desirable assignment. Upstate New York had horrible winters. I, however, accepted the assignment, so I could change aircraft and have the chance to fly more.

I went back to Ft. Rucker, which was good because I got see Marc, Brian, and Kevin. I also qualified as a UH-60 Blackhawk pilot. Then, I was shipped off to Ft. Drum. It just so happened that tension was stirring up in Haiti. The 10th Mountain Division at Fort Drum was sent to sort things out—or at least be one of the significant players in the operation. We qualified for ship landings on the USS Roosevelt aircraft carrier, and a few months later, we sailed down to Haiti on the USS Eisenhower aircraft carrier.

Getting qualified to land on ships and being part of Operations Restore and Uphold Democracy was an interesting experience. The night before the operation began, we went to bed with two rules of engagement: a permissive entry into Haiti or a nonpermissive entry. The difference depended on if we had to fight our way in or not. It turned out that President Carter smoothed things out while we slept. The 82nd Airborne Division turned around in flight. The United States was granted permissive entry. The Haitian government made a wise decision to peacefully work things out.

There was a flurry of excitement on deck the next morning. The entire deck of the Eisenhower was a blur of rotor blades. You could hear the edge in the air boss's voice as he cleared the deck of helicopters for their missions. An aircraft carrier had never lost its jet airwing(s) to Army helicopters, but we thought it was pretty cool. I flew more than eight hours that day, moving supplies and troops to and from the ship.

The most interesting thing happened was while I was waiting my turn to land for more supplies. I flew a Port Delta, which means I flew in circles on the Port, or left, side of the ship while I waited for my turn to land. A Marine Corp CH-53, which is a very large aircraft with three engines, did not have a mission and wanted one. While I flew circles, I heard him request to help in some way. He had a big aircraft that could carry a lot of stuff, so his participation was approved. He landed on the bow, or front deck, of the Eisenhower and loaded with heavy items, which was mostly ammunition.

Helicopter pilots are supposed to do a ten-foot hover, power check, which effectively checks the helicopter performance and its weight. That means, pilots do performance planning, based on current conditions prior to flight, and a ten-foot hover check compares predicted power settings against indicated power settings. If the power setting is higher than predicted, it indicates the cargo is heavier than planned. There is a power setting number that should not be exceeded because that number predicts whether the aircraft will have enough power at higher hover heights that exceed fifty feet. The pilot did not do that and took off into flight. The pilots quickly realized they did not have enough power to keep altitude and started descending toward the water. They were much heavier than they thought.

The pilots tried to increase airspeed to fly out of the bad situation. As aircraft get faster, they become more efficient. The pilots, however, could not fly out. Instead, they hit the water on the port side stern. Every time the pilots tried to pick up to a hover, the aircraft started spinning because the tail rotor could not counteract the extreme torque, so the pilot would set the helicopter back down again. Finally, the flight engineers dropped the large external fuel tanks, which made the aircraft light enough to get back on the deck.

After a few months in Haiti, I was sent back to Fort Drum. I decided to apply for Officer Candidate School (OCS). I still did not have a college degree, only my GED, but I found a loophole that allowed me to apply. I had a university evaluate my military education, which gave me enough college credits to apply to OCS. I was selected and went to Ft. Benning, Georgia.

Refer to lesson twenty-three. God equips the called.

Chapter 20

God Sends Specific People into Your Life

"Friendship is unnecessary, like philosophy, like art ... It has no survival value; rather it is one of those things that give value to survival."
—C.S. Lewis

After OCS, I went back to Ft. Rucker for the Officer Basic Course (OBC), which was required for all lieutenants. While there, I met Joe. He became my lifelong best friend. Joe is from an awesome Italian-American family, and they sort of adopted me. I am thankful for them. During the Officer Basic Course, we had to go through Survival Evasion Resistance and Escape (SERE) Level B training. The training was required for all pilots in flight school due to the risk of being shot down and captured behind enemy lines. We started with at the simulator complex where we did a simulated mission. We broke into teams, and each team was sent to the field to simulate being isolated behind enemy lines. We knew who was on our team before the capture. Joe was one of my teammates, and I got to know him during the exercise.

I knew I would like Joe when I saw him gathering spices from the breakroom before the exercise. We were both home cooks and aware we had to catch and kill a rabbit for the team to eat. Joe gathered what he could and then hid the spices somewhere on his person. During the evasion portion of the exercise, we moved cross country and finally made it to the point in the woods where we had to catch and kill a rabbit. After doing so, Joe brought out the spices and we cooked the rabbit. We were all starving, and anything would be good at that point, but the rabbit was the best ever. Joe relished and ate the liver, which was also spiced. I don't do organs, but he liked it.

We had a class formal dinner at the end of the course. Joe's mom and dad came, and I met them for the first time. Joe asked if I was interested in rooming together in Savannah; we were both assigned there after graduation. I thought it was a good idea, but Joe still had a few weeks of training.

Other than the casual conversation about rooming together, we had not spoken any more about it. When I arrived in Savannah, I went ahead and got a one-bedroom apartment. After a few weeks, Joe called to see if I wanted to still room together. I really didn't want a roommate; I never had one before other than in the barracks, so I told him I already had a one-bedroom. Joe was persistent, though, and asked me to see if apartment management would allow a move to a two-bedroom apartment. I felt like I should do it, even though I did not want a roommate. Reluctantly, I agreed. I didn't think management would allow it, but they did. Moving in with Joe turned out to be a life-altering decision. Joe and his family were sent from God.

Joe has been my best friend and confidant ever since. I don't have a story of something Joe did that changed my life, but I can say that he and his family's friendship altered my life in the most positive way. They showed me what a family can truly be.

Lesson Twenty-Six

Surround yourself with godly people who care for and love you. Some may be there for a season and others for a lifetime.

Being vulnerable with a friend is also important. Friendships need to be more than surface-level. A deeper relationship can be transformational.

"The next best thing to being wise oneself is to live in a circle of those who are" (C.S. Lewis).

"Do not be deceived, 'Bad company ruins good morals'" (1 Cor. 15:3).

Chapter 21

Work Hard

"If you can't fly, then run, If you can't run, then walk, If you can't walk, then crawl, but whatever you do, you have to keep moving forward."
—Martin Luther King Jr.

B eing selected for the 160th SOAR remains one of the greatest professional blessings of my life. It seemed unlikely that I would be selected. Other than flight school, my only education included military schooling, and I was a second lieutenant. Typically, senior captains were selected.

After putting in my application packet for the 160th SOAR and making it through the screening process, I had to go to assessment for the regiment. One of three things would come out of assessment: no thank you, or we are interested but you need more experience, or welcome to the regiment. I was a second lieutenant, but I was also an experienced pilot. I completed a tour in Korea as a Cobra attack helicopter pilot before transitioning into UH-60 Blackhawks and serving in Haiti during Operation Restore/Uphold Democracy.

After a lot of paperwork, a physical, and swimming assessment, I met the instructor pilot, Mickey, for my evaluation. Mickey was a nice enough guy, but I did not get great vibes from him. I don't think he appreciated that I was a second lieutenant trying to get into the Regiment. I spent a few days with him. He evaluated my flight skills and knowledge. The oral evaluation came next. The instructor pilot can ask questions from so many areas, so it was difficult.

We are checked for our ability to consistently and precisely navigate without the use of electronic systems, such as Global Positioning System (GPS). We could only use a map, compass, and clock. We had to navigate to two targets within plus or minus thirty seconds of the time we planned prior to the flight. I excelled in that on the check ride. I hit both my targets within the standard time.

After evaluation, I had to go to the board to find out if I made it into the regiment. The board consisted of the gaining battalion commander, the regiment psych, Mickey, and several others. It was not a pleasant experience. When I left the room, I was glad I didn't need this job. When I reentered the board room, I was surprised to hear I was chosen for the 3/160th SOAR. I became a Night Stalker, which is the undisputed best military helicopter unit in the world.

I found out later that Mickey did not recommend me. By the time he told me, we were pretty close friends and had flown together a lot. Mickey and I are still close friends to this day.

I went back to Hunter Army Airfield and moved down the street to 3/160th SOAR. I got assigned to the S3 operations shop until I went to school. Survival, Evasion, Resistance and Escape (SERE), level C, was my first school. I cannot talk much about the school because I signed a nondisclosure statement. I can say the school was significant, extremely difficult, and brutal in many ways. I ended up going to the Navy's SERE school because the Army's was backlogged. It's debatable about which SERE is more difficult. I attended SERE in Brunswick, Maine, and it was bitterly cold that February.

Even in SERE, God was with me. I did well and was even graduated fifteen minutes early to participate in graduation because of my successes in the brutal part of the course. I often say SERE school is the best school I never want to do again.

The next stop was Green Platoon, for 160th specialized pilot training. Again, I won't talk a lot about this because I don't want to betray the regiment's trust. I'll just say that we learned a lot about first aid, hand-to-hand combat, shooting, and of course specialized flying skills in our "new" aircraft. We spent several months getting trained to reach BMQ (Basic Mission Qualified) status and then were shipped off to our units.

I was assigned to A Company Shadows, 3/160th SOAR. I was a platoon leader for several MH-60 Blackhawks and their crews. I was in that position about a year. It was a steep learning curve for me. At some point, my education, or lack thereof, caught up with me. I was informed I needed my bachelor's degree in order to be promoted to captain. I made it all that way, but it was time to get a college education. I was nervous about that.

I worked hard and leaned on God to get through tough times. I needed a weekend tutor to get through calculus class. When I finished my degree at Embry Riddle Aeronautical University, I was assigned to D/160 SOAR in Puerto Rico. That was one of the best assignments of my career. I traveled all over Latin America and the Caribbean, supporting Special Operations missions. I was a first lieutenant, but since I worked at higher levels and was often around senior officers and briefing ambassadors on my trips, and I was frocked to captain. Being frocked means that I wore the next higher rank but was still paid for the rank I actually was. Eventually, my actual rank caught up. The men I served with in D/160 SOAR and 3/160th were some of the best I have ever served alongside.

Lesson

Refer to previous lesson. God equips who he calls.

Lesson Twenty-Seven

God wants you to work hard. Even though God helps in ways you cannot see, He still wants you to work hard for what you receive. It's rare that God makes things happen fast; most of the time He wants you to go through the process for your personal and spiritual growth. The most rewarding things in life come through hard work.

"Whatever you do, work at it with all your heart, as working for the Lord, not for human masters" (Col. 3:23).

Chapter 22

The Journey Is Part of Your Story: Don't Miss It!

"Focus on the journey, not the destination. Joy is found not in finishing an activity but in doing it."
—Greg Andersen

Shortly after I moved to Puerto Rico, I went to the marina and saw a sailboat for sale. I had never been on a sailboat but decided to buy it. Sails work much like airplane wings or a helicopter's rotor blades. Not too much later, I became the sailing instructor for the Roosey Roads Yacht Club. Then, eventually, I was elected as the Commodore of Roosevelt Roads Yacht Club. While living there, I also did a lot of scuba diving.

I accomplished a lot in Puerto Rico. I led trips all over Latin America and the Caribbean; we supported some of the finest Special Operations forces in the world, including foreign special operations forces. I briefed General Officers and Ambassadors on a regular basis and worked at a high level. I was successful and even attained Fully Mission Qualified Status (FMQ), normally a flying level only Warrant Officers attained. Commissioned officers were normally too busy with administrative and leadership duties to gain enough experience to be an effective FMQ.

One day, my company commander called me into his office. He told me our Regimental Commander (RCO) of the 160th SOAR would visit the unit soon. Since I was the resident water guy: diver, sailor, and unit Operations Officer, he asked me if I could plan a unit swim in Peurca Bay that the RCO could participate in. The RCO was a big swimmer. The swim started on a Roosevelt Roads beach and participants swam to Cabritas Cay, a small island in Peurca Bay.

I was familiar with Cabritas Cay. We spearfished there. It was also near the SEAL compound, which was in Puerca Bay. Having experience there, I knew the tiny island was a lot farther from shore than it appeared. It would be a *long* swim. I also knew a six-foot-long bull shark cruised the island waters. Bull sharks are one of the more dangerous sharks because they are aggressive. My friend, Tom, had a run-in with the shark. Tom was a Navy SEAL of note and had excellent water skills. After Tom speared a fish, the shark went after the fish. SEAL or not, Tom was not about to fight with the shark, so he gave his fish to the shark.

I told my commander about the distance issue and the bull shark, but he didn't seem too concerned about it. He told me to plan it anyway, so I did. I did, however, get the commander to agree to everyone wearing an inflatable vest they could use for floatation if they got in trouble. I felt better about the swim with that added safety feature. I asked one of my NCOs, who was a strong swimmer, to help me as a safety swimmer. Jason and I wore wetsuits for added floatation, and we swam out to the island ahead of everyone else.

I posted Jason on the opposite side of the small cay and told him to take a head count as everyone swam by him. I would count people on the other side as they swam back to the Roosey Roads beach. I saw all the swimmers make their way toward Jason's position. After twenty to thirty minutes the participants swam by me on their way back to the beach. I counted each person, most of them were in a large group, but there were a few stragglers here and there. After everyone came by, I was one swimmer short. The RCO had not come past me. I asked Jason if he saw the RCO. He had.

We both surveyed the area, and there was no sign of the RCO. Jason swam back to let the commander know. I searched the water, the beach of the cay, but could not find him. I started to get worried. I envisioned the bull shark attacking our RCO, who also happened to be a Regimental war hero and an all-around great guy.

After a half hour past, the SEALs launched a small rigid inflatable boat (RIB) to help with our search. My commander launched an aerial crew to search in a Blackhawk. Harbor patrol launched a search effort as well. So, we had a full search and rescue operation underway. We were all really worried.

The RCO separated from the group and accidentally swam to the wrong beach. He told us later that he saw the aircraft, and he figured we were searching for him, but there was not much he could do.

After we all recovered from the near tragedy, I told my commander I could take him, the First Sergeant, and the RCO to *Vieques* in my sailboat. *Vieques* is one of the Spanish Virgin Islands. It was a great place to dive, swim, and catch lobster. The RCO loved the idea, so we set sail the next day for *Vieques*. As we got to the mouth of the Roosey Roads Harbor, I saw black clouds heading our way. I pointed them out to everyone, but I was the only sailor in the boat, so they left the decision to me. I continued to watch the weather and got nervous about it. I finally made the call to turn around, but had waited too long. The rough weather caught us.

I had to reef my sail which means I needed to reduce to sail area because the winds were so high. We got beat up but ended up making it back in pretty good shape to my slip at Roosey Roads. The RCO and my commander were good sports about it, but I felt bad about the two incidents.

Lesson Twenty-Eight

Sometimes we miss the journey because we're focused on the destination. As I reflect on my life, I remember small moments with joy. I reflect on both circumstances and relationships I found along the way.

"I plan to do so when I go to Spain. I hope to see you while passing through and to have you assist me on my journey there, after I have enjoyed your company for a while" (Rom. 15:24).

Chapter 23

One of My Darkest Hours

"I believe there are angels among us, sent down to us from somewhere up above. They come to you and me in our darkest hours, to show us how to live, to teach us how to give, to guide us with a light of love."
—Helen Keller

After leaving Puerto Rico, I went to the Advanced Course, which is now known as the Captains' Career Course, at Ft. Rucker, in Alabama. I went back to the conventional Army, at least for a while. After the career course, I was once again blessed to go back to Hunter Army Airfield (HAAF). I believe God had divine influence because it was unheard of to get such a great assignment twice. That assignment changed the direction of my life.

While serving in both 3/160th SOAR in Savannah and D/160th SOAR in Puerto Rico, I did some pretty special things and worked much higher than my paygrade. My head was a little bigger than it should have been, and I was pretty arrogant and pride filled. I thought it was beneath me to serve in a conventional unit.

I was assigned to the 3rd Infantry Division's Aviation Brigade, which was not bad, at least it was a combat unit. But then the bad news came. I had to serve on the division staff as the Assistant Division Aviation Officer (ADAO) which was, in my opinion, the worst job in the Aviation Brigade. I was mortified. I thought

I should have been given one of the best assault companies. I am actually ashamed of the attitude I had; it was not pleasing to God or indicative of who I really was.

Then September 11 happened, and the war started. The 160th SOAR was already in the fight, and I was stuck in the conventional army. I had no idea when I would get to join the fight, which I really wanted to do. I still had a lot of friends in 3/160th SOAR, and they were just down the road. So, I hung out with them often. They rotated in and out of Afghanistan, so I got to hear the latest. One night, I had too much to drink in downtown Savannah, and I needed to get home. I tried to sit it out until I thought I was sober enough to drive. I got stopped on the way home and charged with driving under the influence (DUI).

The officer took me to the police station, and I spent several hours there. That, however, was not the worst part. The military police picked me up, and they put handcuffs on me again, which I hated. My chain of command was notified, and my career and everything I had worked for was in jeopardy. To make things worse, the brigade commander had a huge say in what would happen to me. He was very interested in preserving his career and not interested in preserving mine.

The news of my arrest spread like wildfire. It was not long until everyone knew what had happened. My peers in the aviation brigade, who probably didn't like me and my attitude to begin with, had another reason to think poorly of me. My life's work was in jeopardy because of my foolishness. That was a very dark time in my life.

As with many other times in my life, God used the DUI to humble me and call me back to His purpose. I started going to church again and mending my relationship with God. Even in the ugliness, God worked on the next phase of my life. God takes all things, even the messy, and uses it for good, if you let Him.

I needed something different in my life and started looking for it. I decided I either needed to become a civilian flight instructor or a scuba instructor. I chose to become a scuba instructor. That path eventually led me to my lovely wife, Christina. I didn't know at the time that God was preparing me to help others.

I did survive my DUI experience. By God's grace, I was promoted to major after the incident was cleared from my permanent record. That rarely happens in the military, and I am so grateful it did. God once again protected me when I did not deserve it. I am also thankful to others, like Bill, who assisted in clearing my record.

Lesson Twenty-Nine

We need God in our darkest hours. We've all heard that God will never let us have more stress or pain than we can handle, but that is misleading. First, God does not cause bad things to happen to us. We also get overwhelmed by things that happen in our lives. Suicides are on the rise, which means people feel they have more than they can handle. The truth is, sometimes we *do* have more than we can handle, but God wants us to lean on Him to get through it. So, when life gives us more than we can handle, God is there for us.

"For in the day of trouble he will keep me safe in his dwelling; he will hide me in the shelter of his sacred tent and set me high upon a rock" (Ps. 27:5).

Lesson Thirty

Pride is a dangerous thing and can lead to your own destruction or someone else's. Humble yourself at every opportunity. My hands can push a broom just as good as they can fly a helicopter. We need to treat everyone the same and not let pride go to our heads. That is another reason to surround yourself with godly people who can hold you accountable in a loving way. C. S. Lewis said, "For pride is spiritual cancer: it eats up the very possibility of love or contentment, or even common sense."

"A person's pride will humble him, but a humble spirit will gain honor" (Prov. 29:23).

Lesson Thirty-One

God's timing is perfect, and God often uses time to develop us for His plans. It's just like Joseph learned how to manage and serve while suffering. Later, he was called to do great things. It took me about twelve years before SEAKERS materialized because God was uniquely preparing me for a ministry that would change people's lives.

"Wait for the Lord; be strong, and let your heart take courage; wait for the Lord" (Prov. 27:14).

Chapter 24
God Pairs You with the Perfect Partner

"Being in love—is not merely a feeling. It is a deep unity, maintained by the will and deliberately strengthened by habit; reinforced by the grace which both partners ask, and receive, from God."
—C.S. Lewis

Christina is the greatest gift God has ever given me. She is an unearned gift from God. I met her as a result of my DUI. God brought goodness and the blessing of Christina even during my foolishness and sin. Our awesome friends, Aaron and Alana, introduced us. I knew Aaron and Alana because I became a scuba instructor. Aaron was a scuba instructor as well. We were also both on the Division Staff. I was the Assistant Division Aviation Officer (ADAO) and Aaron was on the intelligence staff.

Aaron and I both deployed to Operation Iraqi Freedom (OIF) with the 3rd Infantry Division. We were there for several months. We set up in Kuwait and waited for the war to start, which it did a few months after we arrived. Aaron and I grew closer over that time. After several months in Iraq, I was selected to command a company back at Hunter Army Airfield. That was a blessing from God because I got a DUI while in the Aviation Brigade, so I needed my brigade commander to approve the command, which he did.

I went home to Hunter for my command inventories and to take command. I was the commander of Headquarters Company, Garrison, Hunter Army Airfield. Command was an awesome experience. My command included the Garrison staff, parachute riggers, chaplains, and the air traffic control tower. At the time, I owned an AA5 Grumman Traveler, single-engine airplane. I used it to shoot approaches at Hunter for air traffic controller training. At the time, the wars in both Iraq and Afghanistan raged, so military pilots did not want to use some of their precious time to practice approaches for the controllers.

A few months in command, something happened at Ft. Stewart with the Reserve Mobilization Battalion. That battalion handled reservists deployment to OEF/OIF. The soldiers were mistreated, and a large, national investigation ensued. Most of the chain of command was fired, and I was asked to take command of Bravo Company, which had more than two hundred soldiers—in addition to the one hundred soldiers I already had. I had to command the two companies simultaneously. I got busy really quick.

By that point, Aaron was back from Iraq, and I was invited over for a dinner party. A beautiful woman named Christina Bickel was also there. We quickly took a liking to one another and started dating. Christina was also a pilot. She originally flew Blackhawks, like me, before transitioning to the intelligence community to fly fixed-wing RC-12s. That is an intelligence version of the civilian King Air. She was also scheduled to take command of a company at Hunter about the time I was due to finish command.

Before leaving command, I had the opportunity to deploy with my parachute riggers who were attached to 1st Ranger Battalion, 75th Ranger Regiment. I routinely flew with those guys in the 160th SOAR, and I felt blessed to deploy with them. We deployed to Bagram Airfield, Afghanistan, and then I went to a fire base where rangers patrolled the surrounding area. I spent a couple weeks there and tried to earn my keep by doing aviation surveys of the helicopter landing area. It was an interesting deployment. We received indirect fire on a regular basis, but most of it was ineffective.

When I left command, I went back to 3/160th SOAR, which was on Hunter. I also took over the Direct Action Penetrator (DAP) platoon. A DAP is a Blackhawk gunship that is armed with a wing mounted, fixed forward 30mm cannon; two, fixed forward M124 mini guns that shoot up to four thousand rounds a minute; and a nineteen-shot rocket pod. It was a heavily armed aircraft and was devastating to the bad guys on the ground. The DAP could also serve as an assault aircraft that delivered troops on a mission. We dropped the 30mm and rocket pod, and flexed the mini guns out for the crew chiefs to fire as door guns. I began deploying every three or four months to Iraq. I flew both gunship and capture/kill missions on a regular basis.

Christina and I continued to date and quickly fell in love. We built a relationship out of our personal brokenness. Christina has always been a firecracker, quick tempered. Her Army nickname was Spike. I, on the other hand, don't like conflict. So, we struggled a bit as we figured each other out. In reality, God worked to repair both of our brokenness. We got married June 5, 2005. We have issues like everyone else, but with God at the center of our marriage, we continue to work through issues and continue to grow together.

In some cases, sin is generational. That's why families can suffer generation after generation. They carry the sin of their families into their own lives and it travels through each generation. Only those who break away can change their paths.

How do you counteract a generational sin? Start by finding a church. Prior to meeting Christina, I attended Savannah Christian, which is now Compassion Christian. You would be surprised how many Savannah-based Night Stalkers are in attendance. It's a powerful church with an anointed senior pastor and staff.

Christina and I chose to make church a priority. I am not talking about religion or legalistic rules like the Ten Commandments. I'm referring to relationship with God through His son, Jesus Christ. If you can do this one thing, everything else will fall into place.

After leaving command, Christina was reassigned to Florida Southern College in Lakeland, Florida. Separation was a challenge, but we were both used to separations because of wartime deployments. It was something we got through. Christina tried to get a job at a university nearby, but God had other plans. Her move turned out to be a blessing because Marc, my son, got to be under Christina's leadership and supervision in the ROTC at Florida Southern College while he attended college. Once again, God worked through our situation and provided Marc with what he needed at the time.

Lesson Thirty-Two

Having a relationship with Jesus Christ aligns your earthly relationships. It won't resolve all issues. You will still experience challenges, but your situation will improve in all areas of your life.

Lesson Thirty-Three

Both earthly and heavenly relationships take work. They don't happen without work on our part. Going to church with your family, being part of a small group, and reading the Bible and praying are important. You can also improve your relationship with God through service in your church. You can become the hands and feet of God.

"Seek the Lord and his strength; seek his presence continually" (1 Chron. 16:11).

The Five Love Languages

The Five Love Languages by Gary Chapman is one of the best books you can buy to help grow your marriage. If you're not careful, though, you can miss the meaning and value of the book. Christina loved the book, and we used it to help us understand each other and improve our relationship. We misunderstood, however, what we believed to be the message of the book. If you're not careful, you can incorrectly interpret the five love languages: quality time, words of affirmation, acts of service, receiving gifts, and physical touch.

Christina's primary love language is words of affirmation. She craves for people to tell her the value she has or things she does well. She wants to be seen, and being seen meant receiving encouraging words from others. For years, Christina looked to me to "fill her love tank," as the book says. She wanted affirmation from me, and I struggled to give it to her. Christina has a high daily word count she wants to hit. I have a significantly lower daily word count, and my count didn't contain a lot of words of affirmation for her. We both struggled in that area for years.

It took us many years to realize the point of the book was to recognize how other people show us love. It's still important for me to give Christina words of affirmation and for me to show her love in the way she feels love, but she has learned to recognize my love for her through other love languages. I show love through acts of service, such as cooking family meals, making her morning coffee, earning our family's income, and other acts like that. We missed that message the entire time. I showered her and my children with love in ways that were most natural for me. When Christina realized that, she was able to keep her love tank full because she saw I served her and my family.

While *The Five Love Languages* is extremely helpful, it's not the primary place where we should go to find our self-worth. When we look to other people to validate us or tell us who we are or what we're worth, people will always disappoint us. By looking to Christ and finding our identity in Him, we can keep our love tanks full because He doesn't disappoint. He is always near and present.

Lesson Thirty-Four

Recognize how people show you love and look for it regularly. Don't force people to love you only the way you want to be loved. Love comes in many forms. God created us to be unique and we show love in many ways.

Lesson Thirty-Five

People, no matter how much they love you, will disappoint you at some point, even if they do not mean to. Don't look to people to fill your "love tank"; look to Christ.

Chapter 25

Powerlines Are Not a Helicopter Pilot's Friend

"This is why being a helicopter pilot is so different from being an airplane pilot, and why in generality, airplane pilots are open, clear-eyed, buoyant extroverts, and helicopter pilots are brooding introspective anticipators of trouble. They know if something bad has not happened it is about to."

—*Harry Reasoner*

A group of us pulled operational control (OPCON) one night, which meant we attached to our sister unit that had three aircraft and needed a fourth. We were the fourth aircraft in the formation. Those missions almost always involved time-sensitive targets (TST). We went after a High Value Target (HVT) on missions like that. We started our day with breakfast, which was actually dinner because we worked nights, then we preflighted our aircraft and started them up to do our system and maintenance checks. Then we shut the aircraft down and went back through the checklist. We did that because the nature of a TST was to launch as soon as possible after we received actionable intelligence.

Once that was done, we headed to the planning area and did as much preparation as possible. We never knew where we were going, so we had limited things we could do. We checked weather for the surrounding area and prepared our kneeboard package, including crew frequency cards, execution checklists, aircraft performance planning, and so on. We talked with the Flight Lead to get a face-to-face. Crew chiefs did a little maintenance on the aircraft and made sure we were ready to go. The 160th has the best crew chiefs and maintenance personnel a pilot could ask for. They got the job done with little to no direct supervision and were proficient at their jobs. Our crew was very close since we ran a lot of difficult missions together. There is a lot of mutual trust among the crew.

Our normal OPCON routine included binge-watching our favorite TV shows, such as *The Shield* and *Deadwood*. Most nights, we got a call, and all of us ran to the Tactical Operations Center (TOC) and aircraft. Most of the crew went to the aircraft to get the rotor blades turning. One pilot went to the TOC to get information on the mission and any imagery of the target area.

One night, we were all in the OPCON alert room watching *Deadwood*, and a call came in. The crew chiefs and I headed to the aircraft. Mike, the other pilot, went to Mission Planning. After thirty minutes I had the aircraft ready for flight and Mike climbed in. He briefed us on the mission. We flew north of Mosul, to a small town, where we conducted a Direct Action (DA) capture/kill of an HVT. That mission was odd because our landing area was just outside of town. Typically, we landed in the HVTs front yard. That gave us the upper hand on the enemy.

That night, we were to land outside of town, four aircraft in a row. Then the customers would walk to the HVT's house. Mike showed us a set of wires that ran parallel to the landing area, but were not to be an issue.

We departed Mosul Airport as a flight of four MH-60s and headed north to the target. The flight was about forty-five minutes. It was standard procedure to keep aircraft three to five rotor discs separation (about 150–250 feet) from each other. For some reason, the third aircraft in the formation drifted back ten rotor discs separation from the second aircraft in formation. I was in the fourth aircraft in the formation. We discussed the larger-than-normal separation. If aircraft three did not catch up, it would be a problem for us. Pilots always try to land into the wind because it requires less power and since we land into the wind, dirt, sand, debris, and turbulent wind blow toward the aircraft in the rear of the formation. So, pilots plan to land in clear air, which means the last aircraft in formation lands first.

That ten rotor disc separation was problematic for us because it would force us to land last and all the dust would blow our way from the three aircraft ahead of us. Mike and I spoke and considered making a radio call to the third aircraft to catch up. We decided against it, however, because we typically avoided radio chatter during missions. We also knew it would embarrass the third aircraft if we called them out over the radio. Then, aircraft three nosed the aircraft over to catch up. We followed suit, but since we had to react to his flight input, we were delayed in speeding up.

Aircraft three caught up to the other two aircraft just prior to reaching the release point (RP). That caused a bigger problem for us. The RP is the last aerial checkpoint prior to landing, and a lot of things happen at the RP. Aircraft slow from 120 knots to 80 knots and eventually down to zero as they land. Aircraft also make their turn to final for landing. So, the first three aircraft were flying at 80 knots, and I was flying in a bit of a dive at about 150 knots. So, the rate of closure was super-fast. I had to make pretty aggressive control inputs to slow down while trying to figure out how to get on the ground before everyone else. It was too late, though; the other three aircraft beat me to the ground.

I should have gone around to wait for the dust to settle. However, we are taught to not split the ground force if at all possible. If I made a go-around, the men who got off the other aircraft would potentially fight without a quarter of their force. Still, in hindsight,

I should have made a go-around. I was on final approach, looking for my landing area, but it was obscured by dust from the other aircraft. I crosschecked my forward-looking infrared (FLIR) and my night vision goggles (NVGs). Both give slightly different pictures, which helps us see through obscurants like dust. I still had trouble seeing the aircraft in front of me and didn't want to run into them. As I struggled to land, my crew chief shouted "Wires!" Since I was still just above the dust, I saw the previously briefed wires that ran parallel to our landing area.

"Roger, I see them."

Those wires, however, were not the ones he was talking about.

During landing, my crew chief yelled, "Tail up! Tail up! Tail up!" Which meant: Take off now, or you're going to crash. I pulled in power to start coming out, but it was too late. My aircraft was heavy from troops and equipment, so it did not respond fast enough. I was still settling downward. The wires were directly under the helicopter. As I struggled to take off, sparks flew. My aircraft got caught in the powerlines. Then the transformer to the left exploded, which cut power to the entire town. By that point, Mike was on the controls with me, as we often did in times like that. We *finally* started ascending out of the dust and powerlines.

As we rose above the dust, I saw the other aircraft taking off. I was happy to avoid a mid-air crash.

I was not sure which part of the helicopter hit the powerlines. My crew chief said he saw three cut lines, but no one knew which part of the helicopter cut them. If the tail rotor cut them, there was a good chance the tail rotor was damaged, and I would lose control at some point. I demanded a lot of power from the aircraft, and it was still slow and heavy. As we climbed back into the sky, we all waited to see what would happen, but nothing did. It turned out that my tailwheel hit the wires and the tailwheel had a Wire Strike Protection System on it. That system was equipped with a sharp cutting device.

We circled around and landed to let our troops off. That near crash only resulted in us having to change out the tailwheel gear because it had been arched by the electricity from the lines. Yet another very close call.

Lesson

Refer to previous Lesson seventeen; prayers work!

Chapter 26

God Is Present in Death

"None of us are getting out of here alive."
—*R. Alan Woods*

I, like most of you, have experienced death. War-zone deaths and deaths of family members, friends, and pets can be the most heart-wrenching experiences. My grandfather was the first person I was close to, who I lost. My grandfather was the best earthly example I had of a father. His passing was difficult for me. We knew his time was coming because he started to have significant slips in his memory, and we knew he was rapidly decreasing in all aspects of his health. Sometimes death is more tragic than others, but my grandfather's passing was beautiful in many ways. We knew his time was coming, which gave us all the opportunity to mentally prepare. I flew to Florida to be with him in his final hours. God gave that gift to me. I was able to have one last conversation with him and then hold his hand while I sat at his feet as he passed.

My grandmother's passing was similar to my grandfather's; it was not tragic. She died surrounded by loved ones at an old age.

I think many of you can relate to a passing like that. It's a bit easier to see the goodness in it or at least to have peace in it.

My grandfather did good things on this earth, found God's purpose for him, and passed peacefully. That is what we all want for loved ones and ourselves. But it doesn't always happen like that, does it? Sometimes, death comes unexpectedly, and other times it comes through tragedy.

My brother's passing was more tragic than my grandparent's. Not only was Craig my brother, but he was also my friend and such an awesome person. I love him dearly. We had so much in common and spent a lot of time together.

My commander knocked on my door one night while I was deployed to Mosul, Iraq. He told me someone in my family had a heart attack, and he thought it was my brother. Craig was not even two years older than me. At the time, we were both in our thirties. After receiving the information, I went to our mission planning area and called Christina. Craig had a heart attack, and his prognosis was not good. He was playing tennis with my younger sister, Jaime, when it happened. He was awake when he fell to the court, and even lit another cigarette before losing consciousness.

Not all heart attacks are the same. Some result in the heart stopping completely. When that happens, the patient can be kept alive with basic CPR until help arrives. CPR is when someone performs chest compressions that act to mechanically pump the heart and lungs and puts oxygenated air in the lungs with either an oxygen kit or breathing into the patient's mouth. With some heart attacks, the heart goes into fibrillation and the benefit of CPR is much less effective, if not altogether worthless. Heart fibrillation means the heart begins to quake or twitch and needs to be reset with a defibrillator. The defibrillator sends an electrical shock to reset the heart rhythm.

Several defibrillators were nearby at the tennis courts because it was a county park, but no one was trained on them. By the time an ambulance arrived, it was too late for Craig. Paramedics did finally get his heart started again, but they did so after five minutes, and Craig suffered brain damage. Later, he did not show any brain activity.

In a matter of hours, I was on a plane out of Mosul headed to Charleston to get to Craig. He was on life support, and we gathered in the waiting room. We received the bad news that Craig did not have any brain activity. The doctors said there was no hope Craig would recover. The only decisions we had was when we took Craig off life support and if we wanted to donate his organs. That information devastated all of us.

Craig and I were close. I loved my brother very much. We prayed for Craig's full recovery, but it did not come to pass.

I don't have all the answers in this matter of life and death, but I do know God was with us the entire time—even in the painful aftermath. God comforted us all in a time we needed Him. I cannot imagine going through something like that without God's love and support. His ways are subtle, but He is always present.

We all have free will. Craig was a teenager when he chose to smoke cigarettes. By the time he was an adult, he smoked two to three packs a day. He smoked for more than twenty-five years. That significantly contributed to his death. We worried about lung cancer taking Craig at some point, but we did not consider a heart attack. We think he had plaque built up in his arteries from years of smoking, and a piece of that plaque loosened and sent his heart into fibrillation. It probably did not help that he lit a cigarette after he went down on the tennis court either. That clearly explains why he had a heart attack. I will not know why God did not intervene until I get to the other side. I am not sure if Craig's purpose had been fulfilled or maybe his death was meant to serve some purpose. His organs saved several lives; perhaps the organ recipients' purposes had not been fulfilled and they needed more time. I don't know, but God is sovereign even in death.

I think many of us make ourselves the judge of things we will never understand. We get mad at God for not acting when we think He should. I don't know why God spared my life on so many occasions but chose not to save Craig. Some people say God does not answer their prayers. I think God always answers our prayers, but sometimes His answer is "No," or "Not yet."

God's ways are higher than mine. I will not sit on His throne and judge. I can never possibly understand His ways and His purpose for doing what he does. That may seem like a cop out—an easy button—but I believe it. I choose to believe God knows what is best in all situations because I witness it all the time. Why would death be different? I believe there are second and third order effects, many we are not aware of, that support God's decisions. Craig contributed to his own death through poor choices, and most of us get that, but my family struggled to understand why God did not answer our prayers for a full recovery.

Lesson Thirty-Six

We live in a world where bad things happen to good people. My friend and mentor, Pastor Josh, once said in our men's Bible study that sometimes our losses are from other's trickled-down sins, which affect us, too. Sometimes those losses are a result of our own sinful choices.

Lesson Thirty-Seven

No matter how smart we are, we will never have God's wisdom and understanding. Sometimes, God says "No" when we ask Him for something we think is important. Prayers, however, are always answered in some way.

"'For my thoughts are not your thoughts, neither are your ways my ways,' declares the Lord' (Isa. 55:8).

Lesson Thirty-Eight

I know this is cliché, but my brother, and all believers, go to a better place when they die. They are with the Lord and truly do not suffer; they are surrounded with love. Their deaths are not a bad thing for them, but those who are left behind suffer. I miss my brother, but I know I will see him again because we are both believers in the Son of God.

"I am hard pressed between the two. My desire is to depart and be with Christ, for that is far better. But to remain in the flesh is more necessary on your account" (Phil. 1:23–24).

"He will wipe away every tear from their eyes, and death shall be no more, neither shall there be mourning, nor crying, nor pain anymore, for the former things have passed away" (Rev. 21:4).

Chapter 27

The Great Architect

"Whatever good things we build end up building us."
—Jim Rohn

I did not know about the SEAKERS ministry that I would later start during this time in my life, but I thought I would open a scuba shop when I retired from the military. I poured all my time and resources toward that goal. After gaining teaching experience for some time, I started my technical diver training with a great instructor named Bert. Technical diving comprises of a few different disciplines: diving below 130 feet water depth—the recreational limit—diving in overhead environments—caves or shipwrecks—using mixed gasses—helium—decompression diving, and/or using specialized equipment like double tanks, rebreathers, and so forth.

At the time, I had no interest in becoming a cave diver but wanted to extend my depth and time underwater. While completing my training, I got the opportunity to go into a cave system at Manatee Springs in Florida. Bert had a cave instructor candidate and needed a water dummy—student—for the instructor to teach, so he could then evaluate the instructor's teaching. I was already equipped to go into the cave since I was doing technical training anyway, so I agreed and was hooked from then on. I absolutely loved technical diving, including cave diving, so much so that I became a technical diving instructor in almost all areas of technical diving: Trimix (helium), decompression, cave, rebreather, and so on.

After gaining more experience, I decided to dive the Andrea Doria wreck, which is considered the Mount Everest of wreck dives. About eighteen people have died while diving that wreck. The reason it's so dangerous is all the conditions that could make diving dangerous, such as currents, temperature, lighting, and so forth, are present on this single dive. The depth of the wreck is close to 250 feet. The water temperature is close to 40° F. The currents are terrible, and it's pitch black. On top of that, there are shipping lanes around the wreck. Needless to say, it was a difficult dive, but it's one I'll always remember.

I needed to become an instructor trainer to complete my plan. Chris, who later became a friend, completed my instructor trainer certification. I was ready to open a scuba shop. Running a dive store is no easy task. If not done correctly, it's a quick way to the poor house. Many scuba divers turned their passion of diving into their primary means of employment only to be sorry for it later. It's a tough business. Christina, to her credit, said she would support my dream, but I had to draft a real and honest business plan. Well, that proved to be a sound piece of wisdom from my wife. After several months of building the business plan with Aaron, and some help from Kevin, my brother-in-law, I decided the dive shop was no longer a good idea.

The reality of running a dive shop is not the same as being a part-time instructor who got to teach scuba. With running a scuba shop, there was a lot of administrative work and selling gear to pay the bills. After looking at the numbers and the work required, it did not match up with my dream job. So, there I was, an extremely overqualified scuba instructor. I wasted so much time and many resources for a business that I didn't open. That's how God works sometimes. He was preparing me for something different the entire time. All along my journey, the resources and time were there for me to train and prepare. It actually came easy to me, and my progression was rapid. God was not preparing me to open a dive shop. He was preparing me for the ministry I would lead later in my life. I also built a lot of relationships during that time, which have helped us build SEAKERS.

Lesson Thirty-Eight

I often call God the "Great Architect." God's design will always be better than ours. Because of free will, God will not force His design on us. We have to submit to Him and trust Him in order for His design to come through.

"For he was looking for the city which has foundations, whose architect and builder is God" (Heb. 11:10).

Chapter 28

Surrender to the Lord

"It is wonderful what miracles God works in wills that are utterly surrendered to Him."
—Hannah Whitall Smith

O nce I retired from the Army, I got a job at a major port authority. That job was a blessing on many levels. Many of those blessings involved God preparing me for what He had in store for me. I often call God the "Great Architect" because He designs things so much better than we ever dreamed.

The Port Authority prepared me for the next thing God had for me. Yet, I tried to leave as soon as I got the job. My transition from an intense military career to maintenance manager was extremely difficult for me. In the 160th SOAR, everyone wanted to do their best and wanted to be there; we were all volunteers. It was a wonderful place to work, and I felt like I made a difference and got to do something bigger than myself. While the Port Authority was filled with great people who did great work for the community, it was not the same.

I had very little training for my job as Port Fleet Maintenance Manager. As a leader in the Army, I was responsible for my helicopters' maintenance, but I was not a maintainer. I was more of an operator who made sure my aircraft were maintained. In spite of my lack of maintenance experience, God blessed my work.

When I arrived, the fleet maintenance budget was over by a hundred thousand dollars. It wasn't long before my team and I got the budget under control; we came in under budget in the first year. At the same time, our average equipment downtime improved. I had a great team. They helped with the overall fleet maintenance improvement.

We did so well in fleet maintenance that I was asked to take over spreader bar maintenance as well. Spreader bars are devices on large ship-to-shore cranes that latch onto shipping containers and move them from ship to shore or from shore to ship. Spreader bars are a critical piece of equipment, and when they went out of service, we measured downtime in minutes. With God's blessing and direction, and a great team of maintainers, we were very successful. During my three-year tenure as the Spreader Bar Maintenance Manager, spreader bar downtime was reduced from .37 in the first year to .26 in the second year to .18 in the third year. In a business where downtime is tracked in minutes, that was a significant reduction in downtime for the ship-to-shore cranes. Bromma, the spreader bar manufacturer, wrote an article partly on our department's successes. The article was titled, "An American Growth Story."

Later I was asked to take over the Rubber Tired Gantry (RTG) yard cranes. I was promoted to Corporate Safety and Emergency Manager after that. I thrived at work, but I hated the industrial environment. When I say environment, I don't mean the people; they were great. I just was not happy working in maintenance; I missed the Army and the Special Operations community.

From the time I started working at the Port Authority, I tried to find a job I thought I was better suited for. I looked to get back into the defense or public sectors, but I could not find the right job no matter how hard I tried. That continued for five years. I prayed daily that God would deliver me from my job. God was not ready for me to move on though. He had more planned for me. I had to learn certain skills at the Port Authority. I felt my plan was better than God's, and I didn't understand why he let me sit in that job for so long.

Christina and I grew our family during that same time. First came Tucker and then Bradley.

Christina and I also talked a lot about whether we wanted to stay in Savannah or move to be closer to her family in Charlotte, North Carolina. To be able to move, I had to find the right job. We finally submitted to the Lord about my job, which meant we stayed in Savannah. We even found the perfect house right on a tidal creek near the Ogeechee River; it was our dream house. We put in an offer on the house, and it was rejected. Once again, our plan was not God's plan at all.

When Aaron left the Army, he became a realtor. He agreed to waive his fee in order to put our money where it needed to be; then the other realtor did the same thing. Our offer was still rejected. At that point, there was no earthly reason for our home purchase to not work out.

We were exasperated and went to the Lord in prayer. We surrendered both the job hunt and house hunt to Him. We thought we were supposed to stay in Savannah, so why didn't the Lord bless our home purchase? About that time, I received a message from an old Green Beret friend whom I knew from my time in Puerto Rico. He and I both lived on boats in the Roosevelt Roads Marina. He wanted to know if I was interested in a job teaching Special Operations Air Courses for a military university. They wanted a former 160th SOAR pilot who had a graduate degree—minimum of a master's degree but a doctorate was even better. It just so happened that I finished my Master of Aeronautical Science while I was at the Port Authority. I had also started my doctorate. The teaching job required worldwide travel to teach partner nations how to do exactly what I had done while in the Regiment.

As it turns out, God knew what he was doing the entire time. I did not. God required Christina and I to grow through the process.

I had to work on my education so I would be prepared for the job, and Christina and I had to surrender to God's plan. In hindsight, I see that God was preparing me for my next job, which was my dream job and still is.

We also received the blessings that Tucker and Bradley are. Those boys are my pride and joy. Each came into this world in a unique way while I was at the Port Authority.

Lesson Thirty-Nine

Surrender to the Lord. The Israelites stayed in the wilderness for forty years because they did not submit to the Lord. If they had submitted and trusted God, they would have made it to the Promised Land a lot sooner.

I believe I would still be lost in my Port Authority job if Christina and I had not truly submitted to God's will and purpose. Furthermore, the wilderness is part of the purpose. It's a time for God to work on us and prepare us for the next thing we will face. But God does not intend for us to stay in the wilderness. He only wants us to learn from it for a time.

"Trust in the Lord with all your heart, and do not lean on your own understanding. In all your ways acknowledge him, and he will make straight your paths" (Prov. 3:5–6).

Chapter 29

God, Is that You?

"Before you speak, it is necessary for you to listen, for God speaks in the silence of the heart."
—*Mother Theresa*

God communicates in many ways. Most of it is not like what you read about in the Bible. God rarely speaks to someone in a burning bush or through audible speech. He shows up in different ways that are unique to the person He communicates with. My wife hears from God in the form of a heart in nature. Hearts show up all the time, particularly when she needs reassurance from God. God communicates a different way with me. I'll get a subtle, other times intense, feeling of an action I should or should not take.

I received a call from my sister one morning while I was at the gym. My nephew, Josh, who was thirty-two years old, was missing. He left all of his belongings where he was staying, which added another layer to the mystery. Given his history, however, I was not overly concerned when my sister called me. Josh was often in a bind or experienced some sort of trouble. I continued my workout but began to feel like I needed to be involved somehow. The uneasy feeling finally got the best of me. I called Christina and told her about it on my way home. I felt led to drive the three hours to my sister's house and help investigate. I didn't understand why. Josh had only been missing several hours.

When I got home, Christina told me she had the same compelling feeling. We both felt that I should go. By that time, my sister and mother were in full panic. They were convinced Josh killed himself and was in a ditch somewhere.

I got in the car and prayed that Josh would be found before something terrible happened. I planned to take a particular route to my sister's house because it was the fastest and most direct route. My GPS also recommended it. As I got closer to my sister's, however, I felt strongly that I needed take an earlier exit. If I did, I would find Josh.

I shrugged it off at first. I needed the quickest route to my sister's house, which was still forty minutes away. The road I felt I *should* take was a rural road in the middle of nowhere. I, however, was obedient to what I thought God was telling me, and I took the exit. Immediately, I felt better.

After a few miles down the rural road, I saw a man walking alongside the road. He appeared to be a drifter. I drove past him, but something told me Josh was the drifter. I had not seen Josh in a while. He had recently come home from an enlistment in the Army. The man I passed by was covered in facial hair and had huge sunglasses on. The prompting of the Holy Spirit got stronger, so I turned around. The Holy Spirit guided me. I got back to the man but still did not recognize Josh, so I turned around again.

I looped around four times before I decided to stop and speak to the man. I needed to exclude him as being Josh. As soon as I spoke to the man, Josh recognized me. The man was Josh! I got out of my truck and asked him what was going on and told him everyone was looking for him. He said he was leaving. Everyone would be better off without him, including his children. Drawing from my own abandonment, I counseled Josh that leaving was not the right way to handle his situation. He had to break the chain of generational sin. After a while, we both cried and hugged. He agreed to let me take him home. When I called my sister and told her Josh was with me, I had to repeat myself. She could not believe I found him. They searched for hours, and I just happened to take an earlier exit off the highway.

God led me to Josh while he was in the middle of nowhere. I was meant to counsel Josh in a way that perhaps no one else could. Josh stayed at home and is working through things. If I had not been obedient to the Lord's calling, Josh might still be lost.

When the Holy Spirit calls, we must listen and be obedient. Recognizing His voice comes through prayer and a relationship with God.

Lesson Forty

Listen and be obedient to the Holy Spirit. God speaks to us in many ways, but we need to have relationship with Him to be able to hear Him. There is so much noise in the world that it takes extra effort on our parts to hear Him and to recognize His voice.

"My sheep hear my voice, and I know them, and they follow me" (John 10:27).

"Whoever is of God hears the words of God. The reason why you do not hear them is that you are not of God" (John 8:47).

"Be still and know that I am God" (Ps. 46:10).

Chapter 30

SEAKERS: A New Calling

"God did not direct His call to Isaiah—Isaiah overheard God saying, 'who will go for Us?' The call of God is not just for a select few but for everyone. Whether I hear God's call or not depends on the condition of my ears, and exactly what I hear depends upon my spiritual attitude."
—Oswald Chambers

Fifty years ago, the Lord began preparing me to one day build a ministry that would help others. I needed those five decades of preparation. The Lord knew my path. He knew I would experience suffering, but he also knew I would be willing to answer His call. Even by writing this book, I have answered God's call from many years ago. Due to my obedience to God and the prayers of my mother, Christina, and others, I always had an additional layer of divine protection. I should have failed or died multiple times while I was in the military. I escaped death because I had not yet fulfilled God's purpose for my life. If that is not a reason to follow God's plan, I don't know what is. I should be dead now, but I am alive because God wanted me to do certain things, and He prepared me to do them. Christina had a similar calling, and she is a selfless servant of God. She works tirelessly to serve, and she and I work side-by-side in ministry.

I remember being called to ministry at about four years old. As a child, I thought I was meant to be a preacher because that was all I understood about being in the ministry. My young brain thought I would one day stand before a congregation, preaching God's Word. I rejected the idea because I could not see myself as a preacher. I also did not understand where the idea came from. As it turns out, I was not called to be a preacher. God wanted to use me as another type of servant, in a very different type of ministry. I always kept that early childhood calling to myself because I never understood it. Now I believe God was communicating to me that I would serve Him and others.

At SEAKERS Aquatic Adventures, a 501(c)(3) nonprofit, we use scuba diving to reach others. We aim to lift them up and give them hope. One of our goals is to teach a skill and provide job training to disadvantaged youth. Our motto is to "SEEK Christ through His creation through underwater exploration." The ministry makes a difference in so many people's lives.

I came up with the idea a few years before we actually started the ministry. When we moved to Concord, North Carolina, my wife and I got very involved in our new church. We found a home and a place to serve at Crossroads Methodist Church. God led us to that church after a lot of prayer and many visits to other churches.

Christina worked with a wonderful woman of God named MaryAnn. They wanted to create a small group ministry that included activity groups. That was my opportunity to start a scuba diving group for ministry purposes. Initially, I thought I should create a group for church members built around a fun activity that also allowed participants to see God's underwater creation.

Kevin, my brother-in-law, was a key partner in getting this ministry off the ground. Christina and MaryAnn also worked a lot behind the scenes as small group coordinators.

The cost of scuba diving was the biggest challenge. However, since I taught scuba diving in Savannah, I accumulated a lot of equipment over the years. We were able to use all that gear for the ministry. Even with that, the budget was a challenge. It was difficult to keep the cost low for participants. At times, I used money from my family's personal budget to keep things going.

As God always does, He sent someone to me who changed the direction of SEAKERS. Hobart is a teacher at an alternative high school called The Performance Learning Center (PLC). It is a high school for youth who struggle in traditional school settings. While the PLC is not a high school for at-risk youth, the nature of the school attracts many young people who fit the model. Hobart knew a little about my past and thought my story might connect me with some of the PLC students. He was right. Many students suffered far worse than I had during my childhood.

I first visited the PLC as a mentor for kids who were struggling. I served in that capacity for two years with mixed results before it occurred to me that I might be able to help them better through scuba diving. I approached Rindy, the Communities in Schools representative with my idea to provide scholarships to some kids. She thought it was a good idea. Scuba diving would give kids an outlet—something to do. Communities in Schools is an awesome nonprofit that acts as student advocates and helps them throughout their education.

Previously, I had not thought about working with youth, but I felt God calling me, and SEAKERS, in that direction. I was obedient to the call. We offered full scholarships to four students from the PLC in the first year. The scholarship got each student through more than two years of training and hundreds of contact hours.

When I talk about being blessed through serving others, I am reminded of how SEAKERS has blessed my family and me more than the people we served. I could recount many stories of times we have been blessed, but one example I can give you is this: Before we moved to Concord, we spent a lot of time with Christina's sister, Amanda, and her family. We love them and they love us, but the relationship was far from perfect. There was something there that prevented us from the relationship God desired us to have. Amanda and Kevin, among many others, were key in getting SEAKERS off the ground. Through our ministry work, our relationships have blossomed. Kevin is one of my closet friends. Christina and Amanda are closer than ever, and our children thrive because they all get to serve together. Our ministry played a huge part in our family's blessings. God is so good.

Lesson Forty-One

In many ways, discovering God's purpose for your life is a lifelong journey that takes many years—even decades—to be prepared for. My journey is still ongoing. I don't know the end to my story or what else God may call me to do. But whatever it is, my answer is, yes, Lord.

Lesson Forty-Two

Be present throughout your journey. Don't worry about the destination. God's purpose is fulfilled along your journey, not just the destination. While you may be called to help other people, you are part of God's work as well. Don't miss that. During your journey, God works on the people you help, and He works on you.

Chapter 31

Why Doesn't God Give Us What We Want?

Why doesn't God just give us the money for the work he's called us to? If He is the almighty God who is all powerful and omnipresent, that should be easy. That's not how God works. This relates to the lifelong journey I spoke about in the last lesson.

About the time SEAKERS partnered with the PLC, we also grew from a small, church activities group to a 501(c)(3) nonprofit. God called us to bigger things. Tucker and Bradley were too young to dive at ages seven and five, but they were already SEAKERS in many ways. We had to use some personal money to pay the lawyer for incorporating SEAKERS in North Carolina, and there was a girl suffering from paraplegia that we wanted to fund for our Florida trip. Over dinner we were discussing the young lady and discussing ways to raise the money for her trip. Both Tucker and Bradley contributed all of their allowance savings to the cause. During our first board meeting as a nonprofit, I remember talking about what the PLC and other programs would cost and then telling the board that we had about two hundred dollars in the bank—half of it came from Tucker and Bradley.

In SEAKERS, we pride ourselves for working with a small number of people for a long period of time. Our footprint is small, but it's deep. On average, we spend 250 hours with our youth during their first year. We start kids in the pool, doing a try-scuba experience; then they move into a scuba certification class. We take them to advanced classes, such as enriched air breathing gas, rescue, and professional level training as well. We also focus on discipleship. Scuba diving is a tool for us to minister and share God's Word with young people. Most kids in our program elect to be baptized during some portion of their training. The kids continue into near-peer mentors for new youth in the program.

Our small footprint causes unique challenges when it comes to fundraising. Most organizations want to see big numbers when providing a charitable contribution. These numbers often include the number of people served and the number of counties or local cities served. It often does not work in our favor when we compete for funds. Many organizations can serve hundreds and even thousands in a week or other period of time. But we believe our model of serving a few over a long period of time has a ripple effect in the community that blesses many.

The same year, we partnered with the PLC and became a nonprofit, we also applied for a grant to help pay the bills for one year. We had a lot of needs. My equipment was older, and we had to pay for the full scholarships we awarded. The grant we applied for was from a Methodist Church organization that provides grants to organizations that do faith-based work, such as SEAKERS. We asked for twenty-five thousand dollars. Since our staff was made up of volunteers—and still is today—we thought the grant was a sure thing. All of our money goes to programing and maintenance. But we didn't get the grant, and we were crushed. Looking back, that "No" turned out to be a blessing.

I had another divine appointment with a man named Daryl. A mutual friend introduced us one day, and over lunch God provided a new and better way for SEAKERS to thrive. I told Daryl that we failed to get the grant we prayed for and that I did not know how to fund the scholarships we awarded. I learned that Daryl and his family are some of the most giving people I know. He asked the minimum amount it would take to get started. "One thousand dollars to get things going," I said. He agreed to write a check *that* day. That was so important because it lifted me up and gave me hope for the ministry. Daryl's contribution inspired me. A short time later, I was overseas with the military for a month, and I used my time off to reach out to several organizations for help.

First, I contacted Professional Scuba Inspectors/Professional Cylinder Inspectors (PSI/PCI) to see if they were interested in partnering with us. The owners are godly people and run a worldwide cylinder safety organization. I taught for them for many years as an instructor. They jumped on board and offered to provide the materials and certifications for the classes I planned to teach the scholarship recipients.

That led us to be able to teach professional level courses to young people who could then use that education for employment. One of the scholarship recipients wanted to be a firefighter. We were able to teach students how to inspect a self-contained breathing apparatus and scuba tanks a fire department might use. We also taught them oxygen safety and valve repair.

Next, I spoke to the National Association of Underwater Instructors (NAUI), which is one of the best scuba training programs in the world. They partnered with us to reduce material costs for our students. NAUI also agreed to help us in other areas that were critical to our ability to provide professional level training to our scholarship recipients and staff. NAUI has been a great partner in our ministry.

Those new partnerships fit in nicely with our existing partnerships, which included Open Water Adventures (OWA), a wonderful dive shop in the Charlotte area. OWA blesses SEAKERS by providing free air for our classes, as well as other things. Joe, the owner, has selflessly used his business to bless SEAKERS from the beginning. That is significant because the scuba industry can be quite competitive, and it would have been easy for Joe to see us as competitors. Instead, he continues to help us, which directly impacts young people in our area in positive ways.

The West Cabarrus YMCA allows us to use its pool for scuba classes. The YMCA has been with us since the beginning and has blessed our ministry and blessed their community. The YMCA staff are phenomenal and go out of their way to bless others.

Lesson Forty-Three

God gives us what we need, not what we want. If SEAKERS had received the Methodist grant, one year's budget would have been taken care of, but God had a better and more sustainable plan. God's divine appointment led us to partnerships that have sustained us for years. A quick fix is not always the best thing. God's process is better, but His process takes time and effort, and the willingness to stick with God's plan.

Lesson Forty-Four

The fundraising journey is actually part of ministry. It allows a team to engage in the community, and donors get to partner with you in the Lord's work. It provides an opportunity for people to be part of your ministry through gifting, which helps develop deeper relationships.

"When you are praying, don't say meaningless words like the Gentiles do, for they think they will be heard because of their wordiness. Don't be like them, because your Father knows what you need before you ask him" (Matt. 6:7–8).

We have developed the SEAKERS truths, a borrowed concept from the Special Operations Forces (SOF) Truths. These truths help us focus on what's important. It shapes our worldview and how we interact with the community.

Christ, not Scuba, is the center of our ministry.

SEAKERS will be led by the Spirit, through prayer, and not driven by secular culture and norms, except where required by law.

Relationships and humility underscore everything we do.

People are more important than statistics.

Quality is more important than quantity.

Conclusion

I f you're reading this book because you are going through a tough time in your life, or maybe your entire life has been a challenge, I am sorry you are suffering. If you bought this book because there is something missing in your life and you're looking for answers, I am so glad you read our book. Either way, I hope this book provides hope and reignites your journey toward a more hope- and love-filled life.

Life is not easy. We are meant to find our way through God's help. Ideally, we start our journey by learning who our Creator is and learning to love Him. Then, we learn to love one another as He commands us to do. You are also here to be loved by Him. God loves you unconditionally. You build a relationship with God by seeking Him. In order to fully realize His transformational love, you must seek Him. It is an active relationship and leads to transformation. As you love Him, you will find a way to more deeply love others — even those who persecute you.

Have gratitude in all things. Possessing an attitude of gratitude underscores your relationship with God and others. It sets the tone for how you view the world. It affects your joy, contentment, and relationships.

We have things to work on during our spiritual growth, such as forgiveness, discontentment, selfishness, anger, resentment, habitual sin, and generational sin. Spiritual growth has a lot to do with overcoming sin issues. We all have them, and each one of us should work to overcome habitual sin. We will all fall short at times because we're human. Soul work is not easy work, but it's key to receiving God's full blessing. We cannot live in unaddressed, sinful situations and still receive God's full blessing and protection. We cannot hate people and refuse to forgive, and expect God to show up in our lives whenever we call on Him. Loving and forgiving more comes a lot easier when we actively work on our relationships with Him. It becomes more natural, and He will help you, but only if you let Him.

It would be much simpler if we could learn and apply these lessons early and effectively in life. It often does not work that way because we are in a fallen world that is filled with hate and sin that often affect us in real and tangible ways. However, by surrounding ourselves with godly people, reading the Bible, and serving in our local churches, we can help ourselves.

Our purposes come directly from God and are kingdom purposes. God leads you to yours if you let Him. He uniquely prepares you for what He's called you to do. Preparation is required on your part and is meant to grow your skill set, your mind-set, and your heart. He also provides unearned gifts to help you. When you're good at something, that's a gift from the Holy Spirit. God gifts you with talents that are often key components to what He's called you to do with your life. You have a vote, and God is a gentleman. If you don't want Him involved or if you push Him out of your life, He will bow out. Please don't do that. Stay on your journey, and you will be blessed beyond measure. God's plans for you will always be better than your plans. Oftentimes, God's way look radically different than yours. God is the Great Architect!

The key to it all is to submit to God. If you do that, a lot of what I spoke about in this book will fall into place in your life. I pray that you're blessed by this book and that you find God's purposes in your life. I pray that you learn to fully love and to be fully loved in return.

Life-Changing Invitation

I want to invite you to come to know Jesus Christ as your Lord and Savior. Before I do that, let me tell you a little about Him and why He came to save us.

God is part of a trinity: God the Father, God the Son, and God the Holy Spirit. He is one God in three different forms. That may be difficult to understand, so let me use the example of water. Water can appear in three different forms: liquid, gas, and ice. All three are still H_2O.

God created us, so He could love us and for us to be His people. We rebelled against His authority in the Garden of Eden. We have rebelled ever since. Our sin separated us from God. In return, He gave us laws and a way to reconcile our sin through offerings. Those offerings included a blood sacrifice, such as animal blood. That was not wasted in any sense and was an early form of tithing. The meat from the sacrifice fed the priest in service to God. God also gave us the Ten Commandments to live by. We all still fall short, so God sent His Son as a living sacrifice—the Lamb of God.

Jesus came to Earth to serve and teach about the kingdom of God and to be an example for us to follow. He is the Messiah prophesied about in the Old Testament and the Hebrew *Torah*. Jesus came to take the sins of the world upon Himself. He came to forgive our sins. Jesus shed His blood on a cross on Calvary. That's why we call Him the Lamb of God. Jesus paid our debts. He died on the Cross and rose from the dead three days later. Then, He went to the Father in heaven where He has been given all authority over us.

I am here to testify that Jesus is real. I know Him. As you have learned from my story, God has been active throughout my life. He helped me through hard times. He is the reason for any success I have and is the reason I serve others now. In fact, God is the reason we serve you through this book.

If you want to change your life in the most positive way, accept Jesus into your life by saying this prayer:

Jesus, I have tried this on my own for far too long. I am a sinner and can do nothing good apart from you. I confess my sins to you and accept you as my Lord and Savior. I believe you died on the Cross for my sins and that you rose from the dead on the third day. Thank you for your love, grace, and mercy. Amen.

Find a church you love and get some support for the journey you just started.

I would also like to invite you to partner with us in ministry. We are looking for a scuba gear manufacturer, corporate sponsors, and monthly financial contributors. We have run SEAKERS from our home office and garage for a long time and need to move into an office. Visit https://seakers.org/donate to make a tax deductible donation. One hundred percent of donated funds go into program-ming. Our staff is volunteer-based. By gifting to our ministry, you are our partner in the Lord's work.

Be blessed.

All the Life Lessons in one Spot!

Introduction
Lesson One

Love God and each other above all else. God's greatest commandment to us is to love Him with all our hearts and souls, and then to love one another. This is foundational to all things good in life.

Lesson Two

In order to receive God's blessings and protections, you must seek Him. You must seek God, and He will hear you, and He will bless your life in more ways than you can imagine.

Lesson Three

Attitude is everything. More specifically, having an attitude of gratitude sets the tone for everything. Being thankful, even in moments of struggle, is critical to both your own joy and also your relationship with Christ. It's believing—truly believing—that God does all things for His purpose and your good. He cares, even about the smallest details of your life. If given the opportunity, He will bring good in all things, even situations that are difficult or horrible. Trust God in your bad times.

Be Present
Lesson Four

Be present. You never know the impact you can have on someone. You could change someone's life, and you may never know it. Be present with the people you love and show them what *right* looks like.

Predictions
Lesson Five

Your past does not have to predict your future, but it can if you let it. It can also predict the future for those you love in both positive and negative ways. Your negative life lessons provide an opportunity for change. Generational sins must be broken, or they will continue. The only way to break the cycle is through a personal relationship with Jesus Christ. He is the breaker of the chains that bind and define us.

Forgiveness
Lesson Six

Unconditional forgiveness is the key to having an abundant and joyful life. Forgiveness is more for the person who forgives than for the person receiving forgiveness. Carrying around anger and resentment has a way of stealing the joy from your life. Forgive and move on. It may take conscious effort or even years of reaffirming your forgiveness, but eventually your heart will follow. Not forgiving others can lead to hate, anger, jealousy, and even feeling physically sick. A lack of forgiveness can also steal from other relationships and leave you empty and joyless. Our other relationships suffer as we carry around anger, resentment, and unresolved issues.

Irrational Fear

Lesson Seven

We do not need to fear anything when we allow God to be in control of our lives. He will provide for our needs and protect us.

How Many Times Do You Forgive?

Lesson Eight

How many times do you forgive someone? As many as it takes, but you may want to limit your exposure at some point. My biological father did some horrible things to us, but we are commanded to forgive because we are forgiven. By forgiving him, I don't carry hate around with me, but I also have chosen not to expose myself to him and his behavior anymore.

Lesson Nine

Forgiving someone does not mean you have to have a relationship with them; it means you let go of past hurts. You remember without anger. So many people struggle with forgiveness because they don't fully understand what it means or what it *can* mean. When you forgive someone, you forgive a hurt or action. You are not expecting that everything will go back to the way it was. I also learned that I probably should have decided to end the relationship with my father long ago, and I could have prevented more hurt in my life. Either way, though, I chose to forgive him.

This leads me to the next life lesson that is related to being a follower of Christ.

Lesson Eleven

Christians are not perfect. I often hear people say Christians are hypocrites because they do things the Bible tells us not to do. My previous pastor in Savannah, Georgia, used to say that if we put our faith in him, he will disappoint us one day—not because he wants to but because he is human and will let people down. We all fall short of God's commandments. Our goal is not to sin, but we all do and that does not make Christians hypocrites; it makes us human. Having said that, we should repent and end patterns of sin.

Lesson Twelve

Serving others helps you more than it helps the people you serve. I often heard from people who went on mission trips that they got more out of the trip than the people they helped. I never understood that until I took my first short-term mission trip. I was filled with hope, joy, and appreciation during my trip and when I returned home. There is something about helping others that gives us a sense of purpose, love, and hope. The same thing happens when we serve our communities or our families. Relationships are born, and purpose is given. While church attendance is not the only way to serve others, it does provide a lot of opportunity to do so. For Christians, it also allows us to serve in the context of Christ and even provides opportunities to share the gospel.

Invitation

Lesson Thirteen

Invite someone to church. An invitation to church can be life-saving for someone, and the ripple effects from that simple invitation can be significant.

God Wants You to Dream

Lesson Fourteen

God wants you to dream about a better day and a better way but in the context of His purpose. Some dreams come from God if you let them. The Holy Spirit inspires and guides you—if you let it.

Your Purpose Can Still Be Fulfilled in an Unfulfilling Job

Lesson Fifteen

Sometimes you have to work a job that may not meet your expectations before you can earn a better position. Starting from the bottom is not all bad, and God often has some things for you to do to prepare you for the next and bigger thing. Like my friend, Pastor Lowell, from Crossroads Church says, "Sometimes God makes things happen now, but most of the time He brings you through a process because there is something you need to learn."

God Is Sovereign Even in Your Bad Decisions

Lesson Sixteen

Just because you stray from God's purpose and make poor decisions, that does not mean God abandons you in your foolishness. God gave you free will, and you'll sometimes make bad decisions. God still loves you and can work in your new situation if you let Him.

Prayers Work!

Lesson Seventeen

Prayers are powerful; pray hard for the ones you love. When my mother dies, I may not be far behind because I think her prayers for me have kept me alive on many occasions. Don't underestimate the power of your prayers. Thank you, Mom and Christina, for your constant prayers.

Divine Appointments

Lesson Eighteen

Divine appointments are real; don't miss them. God puts people in our paths who we need, or sometimes they need us.

Be Obedient

Lesson Nineteen

Be obedient when God gives you direction and opportunity. We have free will and can elect not to follow God's prompting, but we will miss a lot of the goodness He has for us if we do.

I had plenty of reasons to avoid all the work that went into my flight packet. The odds of getting in were stacked against me. The reality, however, was I should not have been picked.

Lesson Twenty

Lean not on your own understanding, but trust in God's plan. Do not make assumptions about what God can or will do. Our God is not bound by space and time. He knows what you will need before you ask Him.

Rational Fear: God Is Still Sovereign

Lesson Twenty-One

Rational fear is good because it forces us to react in ways that preserve life, but it is also real that you could lose your life. God is sovereign when it comes to rational fear and life-threatening situations. I believe I was protected because my purpose had not yet been fulfilled. God still had work for me to do, and He knew I would be obedient in His calling. I also had prayer warriors, including my mom, praying for me.

The Story of the Rose

Lesson Twenty-Two

God speaks to us in many different ways, but we have to listen for Him. We have to seek Him in our daily lives. If we do, He will show up in big and meaningful ways. Sometimes we have to wait to understand something God puts on our hearts. When you receive a message from God, write it down or use some other way to remember it. God may use it when we least expect it. Sometimes we have to stop and smell the roses.

God Equips You for His Calling

Lesson Twenty-Three

God will equip you for His work and your purpose. That does not mean you won't have to work hard. It won't happen overnight, but it can. You have to seek God and be obedient to Him. Don't pass up God's blessings because you don't feel you're equipped to fulfill them. God will equip you for His calling.

Forgiveness (Again) and Grace

Lesson Twenty-Four

None of us deserve anything good, but I am so thankful I didn't get what I deserved. God's grace is awesome. Since we receive grace so often, we should give it often.

Lesson Twenty-Five

We must deal with the garbage in our lives and not always blame things on another person's faults. It's easy to blame someone else for all the bad things in our lives, but it's more useful to examine your own role in the conflict and address it. Sometimes we can achieve that between God and ourselves, but sometimes our actions need to be brought into the light, particularly when other people are involved or have been hurt. Sometimes, we need to confess our sins to our heavenly Father, as well as those we have hurt.

God Sends Specific People into Your Life

Lesson Twenty-Six

Surround yourself with godly people who care for and love you. Some may be there for a season and others for a lifetime. Being vulnerable with a friend is also important. Friendships need to be more than surface-level. A deeper relationship can be transformational.

Unearned Gifts

Lesson Twenty-Seven

God wants you to work hard. Even though God helps in ways you cannot see, He still wants you to work hard for what you receive. It's rare that God makes things happen fast; most of the time He wants you to go through the process for your personal and spiritual growth. The most rewarding things in life come through hard work.

The Journey Is Part of Your Story: Don't Miss It!

Lesson Twenty-Eight

Sometimes we miss the journey because we're focused on the destination. As I reflect on my life, I remember small moments with joy. I reflect on both circumstances and relationships I found along the way.

One of My Darkest Hours

Lesson Twenty-Nine

We need God in our darkest hours. We've all heard that God will never let us have more stress or pain than we can handle, but that is misleading. First, God does not bad things to happen to us. We also get overwhelmed by things that happen in our lives. Suicides are on the rise, which means people feel they have more than they can handle. The truth is, sometimes we *do* have more than we can handle, but God wants us to lean on Him to get through it. So, when life gives us more than we can handle, God is there for us.

Lesson Thirty

Pride is a dangerous thing and can lead to your own destruction or someone else's. Humble yourself at every opportunity. My hands can push a broom just as good as they can fly a helicopter. We need to treat everyone the same and not let pride go to our heads. That is another reason to surround yourself with godly people who can hold you accountable in a loving way. C. S. Lewis said, "For pride is spiritual cancer: it eats up the very possibility of love or contentment, or even common sense."

Lesson Thirty-One

God's timing is perfect, and God often uses time to develop us for His plans. It's just like Joseph learned how to manage and serve while suffering. Later, he was called to do great things. It took me about twelve years before SEAKERS materialized because God was uniquely preparing me for a ministry that would change people's lives.

God Pairs You with the Perfect Partner

Lesson Thirty-Two

Having a relationship with Jesus Christ aligns your earthly relationships. It won't resolve all issues. You will still experience challenges, but your situation will improve in all areas of your life.

Lesson Thirty-Three

Both earthly and heavenly relationships take work. They don't happen without work on our part. Going to church with your family, being part of a small group, and reading the Bible and praying are important. You can also improve your relationship with God through service in your church. You can become the hands and feet of God.

The Five Love Languages

Lesson Thirty-Four

Recognize how people show you love and look for it regularly. Don't force people to love you only the way you want to be loved.

Love comes in many forms. God created us to be unique and we show love in many ways.

Lesson Thirty-Five

People, no matter how much they love you, will disappoint you at some point, even if they are not meaning to. Don't look to people to fill your "love tank"; look to Christ.

God Is Present in Death

Lesson Thirty-Six

We live in a world where bad things happen to good people. My friend and mentor, Pastor Josh, once said in our men's Bible study that sometimes our losses are from other's trickled-down sins, which affect us, too. Sometimes those losses are a result of our own sinful choices.

Lesson Thirty-Seven

No matter how smart we are, we will never have God's wisdom and understanding. Sometimes, God says "No" when we ask Him for something we think is important. Prayers, however, are always answered in some way.

Lesson Thirty-Eight

I know this is cliché, but my brother and all believers, go to a better place when they die. They are with the Lord and truly do not suffer; they are surrounded with love. Their deaths are not a bad thing for them, but those who are left behind suffer. I miss my brother, but I know I will see him again because we are both believers in the Son of God.

The Great Architect

Lesson Thirty-Eight

I often call God the "Great Architect." God's design will always be better than ours. Because of free will, God will not force His design on us. We have to submit to Him and trust Him in order for His design to come through.

Surrender to the Lord!

Lesson Thirty-Nine

Surrender to the Lord. The Israelites stayed in the wilderness for forty years because they did not submit to the Lord. If they had submitted and trusted God, they would have made it to the Promised Land a lot sooner.

I believe I would still be lost in my Port Authority job if Christina and I had not truly submitted to God's will and purpose. Furthermore, the wilderness is part of the purpose. It's a time for God to work on us and prepare us for the next thing we will face. But God does not intend for us to stay in the wilderness. He only wants us to learn from it for a time.

God, Is That You?

Lesson Forty

Listen and be obedient to the Holy Spirit. God speaks to us in many ways, but we need to have relationship with Him to be able to hear Him. There is so much noise in the world that it takes extra effort on our parts to hear Him.

SEAKERS: A New Calling

Lesson Forty-One

In many ways, discovering God's purpose for your life is a life-long journey that takes many years—even decades—to be prepared for. My journey is still ongoing. I don't know the end to my story or what else God may call me to do.

Lesson Forty-Two

Be present throughout your journey. Don't worry about the destination. God's purpose is fulfilled along your journey, not just the destination. While you may be called to help other people, you are part of God's work as well. Don't miss that. During your journey, God works on the people you help, and He works on you.

Why Doesn't God Give Us What We Want?

Lesson Forty-Four

The fundraising journey is actually part of ministry. It allows a team to engage in the community and donors get to partner with you in the Lord's work. It provides an opportunity for people to be part of your ministry through gifting, which helps develop deeper relationships.

About the Authors

Shannon McAteer is a Christian, husband, and father to five boys. He is also the Executive Director and Founder of SEAKERS Aquatic Adventures Inc. He lives in Concord, North Carolina. Shannon spent twenty-two years in the United States Army—fifteen of those years were spent as a helicopter pilot. He flew UH-1 Hueys, AH-1 Cobras, and the UH/MH-60 Black Hawks. He spent eleven years with the 160th Special Operations Aviation Regiment (SOAR). After retirement, Shannon taught Special Operations Aviation in support of the United States Special Operation Command (USSOCOM). He is an adjunct professor for a national university. Shannon's studies include a Bachelor of Science degree and a Master of Science degree in Professional Aeronautics, as well as a Doctor of Philosophy in Public Policy.

Christina McAteer is a devoted christian, wife, mother, sister, aunt, and daughter. She is also Vice President of SEAKERS Aquatic Adventures, Inc. Christina graduated from the Reserve Officer Training Corps with a Bachelor of Arts in Communications from Campbell University. She was commissioned as a U.S. Army Aviation Officer in 1997 and spent five of her ten years in the Army as a helicopter pilot and the other five as a fixed-wing pilot. She flew UH/EH-60 Black Hawks and RC-12D/N Guardrail, Signals Intelligence Fixed Wing Aircraft. Christina finalized her Army career as an Assistant Professor of Military Science at Florida

Southern University where she was awarded ROTC Instructor of the Year. Since her Army career, Christina has dedicated her life to volunteering and helping the community. She spent the last seven years volunteering full time at Crossroads Church in Concord, North Carolina, working specifically with small groups, interest groups, curriculum, and adult spiritual education. In addition, she serves on the board of her sons' Parent, Teacher, Community, Organization. God gave Christina a passion for encouraging others. She helps people not only see, but also believe in themselves and their abilities. When her husband, Shannon McAteer, started using his God-given passion for scuba diving to mentor, encourage, and lift others up, she knew God was using scuba diving as a vehicle to transform her life and the lives of many others through the SEAKERS ministry. Christina feels blessed to be part of God's plan for her and her family.

CPSIA information can be obtained
at www.ICGtesting.com
Printed in the USA
LVHW012034070620
657583LV00006B/763